Patron

HER MAJESTY T

Presider

HER MAJESTY QUEEN ELIZABE

Members of the Board

SIR THOMAS ARMSTRONG, M.A., D.MUS.OXON., HON.R.A.M., F.R.C.M.
Principal of R.A.M.

KEITH FALKNER, F.R.C.M., HON.R.A.M. *Director of R.C.M.*

FREDERIC R. COX, O.B.E., M.A.OXON., HON.R.A.M., HON.R.C.M.
Principal of R.M.C.M.

HENRY HAVERGAL, M.A.OXON., B.MUS., HON.D.MUS.EDIN., HON.R.A.M., HON.R.C.M. *Principal of R.S.A.M.*

MYERS FOGGIN, F.R.A.M., HON.R.C.M.

HERBERT HOWELLS, C.B.E., D.MUS.OXON., F.R.C.M., HON.R.A.M.
King Edward Professor of Music, University of London

ANGUS MORRISON, F.R.C.M.

MAX PIRANI, HON.R.A.M.

LESLIE REGAN, B.MUS.OXON., F.R.A.M.

CUTHBERT SMITH, B.A.OXON., F.R.C.M.

JOHN STAINER, B.A., MUS.B.CANTAB., F.R.C.M.

Secretary

WILLIAM COLE, D.MUS.LOND., F.R.A.M., F.R.C.O.

Deputy Secretary

C. M. THORMAN, B.A., LL.B.CANTAB.

Assistant Secretaries

Examinations Manager
R. R. PENNINGTON

Publishing Manager
D. J. REEVES

Central Office

14 BEDFORD SQUARE, LONDON, W.C.1

Examiners to the Board

As at 1st June, 1963

c Kenneth Abbott, D.Mus.Lond.
a, b Arthur Alexander
Maurice Allen, B.A., B.Mus.Oxon.
c John Alston, T.D.
a William Alwyn
Nettie Anderson
c, d Norman Andrew, D.Mus.Manch.
Sibell Archdale
c Robert Ashfield, D.Mus.Lond.
Jean Ashton
Dorothea Aspinall
Richard Austin
Leo Baker, D.F.C., M.A.Oxon.
b, c G. Thalben Ball, D.Mus.Cantuar.
Martie Ball
Sheila Barlow
Sydney Barlow
a, c Kenneth Barritt, D.Mus.Dunelm.
Edwin Benbow
R. Sterndale Bennett, T.D., M.A.Cantab.
Garth Benson
c Claud Biggs
Ronald Biggs
c John Birch
Margaret Bissett
Heather Black
c Leonard J. Blake, B.Mus.Lond.
b, c John Dykes Bower, C.V.O., M.A., Mus.B.Cantab., D.Mus.Oxon.
a, c Malcolm Boyle, B.Mus.Oxon.
David Branson
d Michael Brierley
a Frank Britton
Henry Bronkhurst
Diana Budd
Barbara Bunch
c Allan W. Bunney, D.Mus.Lond.
c Herrick C. W. Bunney, B.Mus.Lond.
Peter Burges, B.A.Oxon.
a Alan Bush, B.Mus.Lond.
c A. V. Butcher, M.A., D.Mus.Oxon.
Andrew Byrne, D.Mus.Lond.
Philip Cannon
c Derrick Cantrell, M.A., B.Mus.Oxon.
Edgar Carr
Graham Carritt, M.A.Oxon.
c, d Eric Chadwick
a Russell Chester, B.A.Lond.
c John Churchill, B.Mus.Lond.
a John Clapham, D.Mus.Lond.
Derek Clare
a, c R. H. Clifford-Smith, M.A.Oxon., D.Mus.Lond.
Gordon Clinton
Greta Colson
John Colson, B.A.Cantab.
Cecil Cope
a Patrick Cory
Miles Coverdale
Christopher Cowan, M.A., B.Mus.Oxon.
a, c Noel Cox, B.Mus.Lond.
c Philip Cranmer, M.A., B.Mus.Oxon.
Harold Craxton, O.B.E.
Lamar Crowson
Geoffrey H. Crump, M.A.Cantab.
a, c Lionel Dakers, B.Mus.Dunelm.
Thomas Dance
b, c Harold Darke, M.A.Cantab., D.Mus.Oxon.
c Denys Darlow
Ivor Davies, M.A.Oxon.
c T. Alan Davies, T.D., M.A.Oxon.
J. A. Davison, M.A.Cantab.
c Hubert Dawkes, B.Mus.Lond.
c Christopher Dearnley, M.A., B.Mus.Oxon.
Norman Demuth
a Ivey Dickson
C. H. Stuart Duncan
John Dyer, B.Mus.Lond.
a Gwynne Edwards
Robert O. Edwards, B.Mus.Lond.
Roy Ellett
Robert Elliott
c Wilfred Emery, B.Sc.Bristol, B.Mus.Lond.
b Keith Falkner
Sidney Fell
b Thomas P. Fielden, M.A., B.Mus.Oxon., D.Mus.Edin.
Cornelius Fisher
a Myers Foggin
a Watson Forbes
c Leon Forrester, Mus.D.Manch., Mus.B.Dunelm.
a Ivor R. Foster
c D. G. A. Fox, O.B.E., M.A., B.Mus.Oxon., D.Mus.Edin.
c Peter Racine Fricker, Hon.D.Mus.Leeds.
Lilian Gaskell
d Dora Gilson
c Arnold W. Goldsbrough
a Eric Grant, B.Mus.Lond.
c Willis Grant, D.Mus. Dunelm.
d Gordon Green
c R. Arnold Greir, O.B.E.
c Eric Gritton
a Olive Groves
Douglas Guest, M.A., Mus.B.Cantab.
c George Guest, M.A., Mus.B.Cantab.
b Patrick Hadley, M.A., Mus.D.Cantab.
Richard Hall
Maurice Hardy
c Eric Harrison
Henry Havergal, M.A.Oxon., B.Mus., Hon.D.Mus.Edin.
a, c Douglas Hawkridge
a Michael Head
c G. H. Heath-Gracie, B.Mus.Dunelm.
Wight Henderson
a, c Douglas Hopkins, D.Mus.Lond.
b, c Herbert Howells, C.B.E., D.Mus.Oxon.
c Sir Percy Hull, D.Mus.Cantuar.
c Raymond Humphrey, B.Mus.Lond.
a John Hunt
a Harry Isaacs
a Frederic Jackson
b Gordon Jacob, D.Mus.Lond.
Roy Jesson, M.A., B.Mus.Oxon.
a Alban G. H. Jeynes
J. Barham Johnson, M.A., Mus.B.Cantab.
Kenneth Jones
a Guy Jonson
Muriel Judd
c Ivor Keys, M.A., D.Mus.Oxon.
Thea King
Colin Kingsley, Mus.B.Cantab.

b Herbert H. Kinsey
Hilda Klein, B.E.M.
d Clifford Knowles
Louise Lamigeon
C. S. Lang, D.Mus.Dunelm.
a Vivian Langrish
Joan Last
a Peter M. S. Latham, M.A., B.Mus.Oxon.
c Richard Latham
Winifred Law
c Geoffrey N. Leeds, D.Mus.Oxon.
Iris Lemare
b, d C. Thornton Lofthouse, D.Mus.Dublin.
a Terence Lovett
David Lumsden, Ph.D.Oxon., M.A., Mus.B.Cantab
Mary Lynch
H. J. McCurrach, M.A., Mus.B.Cantab.
David Mackie
Jean Mackie
b, c Sir William McKie, M.V.O., M.A., D.Mus.Oxon.
b Kathleen McQuitty
a Gwendolen Mason, O.B.E.
b Frank Merrick
a John Milne, B.A., B.Mus.Oxon
Freda Monk
c Reginald Moore, B.Mus.Dunelm.
b Angus Morrison
H. C. C. Moule, M.A., Mus.B.Cantab.
David Moule-Evans, D.Mus.Oxon.
a Dennis Murdoch
a A. Brian Nash
a Constance Newell
J. Morgan Nicholas
C. L. Nightingale, B.A.Cantab.
Sydney Northcote, D.Mus.Oxon.
c Reginald Oakley
Raymond O'Connell
c Harrison Oxley, M.A., B.Mus.Oxon.
Peggy Page
David Parkhouse
John Pauer
a, c Leslie D. Paul, M.A., B.Mus.Oxon., D.Mus.Edin.
Harvey Phillips
Max Pirani
Thomas B. Pitfield
Harry Platts
Joan Plewman
c Shackleton Pollard, B.Mus.Dunelm.
a Ross Pratt
c Arthur J. Pritchard, D.Mus.Dunelm.
W. D. Pritchard, M.A., Mus.B.Cantab.
a, d Ruth Railton, O.B.E., LL.D.Aberdeen
a Priaulx Rainier
a,b,c Ernest Read, C.B.E.
a, c Leslie Regan, B.Mus.Oxon.
a Alan Richardson
a Arnold Richardson
Paul Rogers, M.A., Mus.B.Cantab.
c Colin Ross
Alan Rowlands, M.A.Oxon.
John Rule
John Russell, B.A.Dunelm.
John Rust, M.A., Mus.B.Cantab.
Irene Sadler
Meriel St. Clair
c Cyril L. Salmons
Patrick Savill, M.A., Mus.B.Cantab.
c John Sealey, B.Mus.Dunelm.
a Stanley Shale
Cedric Sharpe
Bernard Shore, C.B.E.
Basil Smallman, M.A., B.Mus.Oxon.
b Cuthbert Smith, B.A.Oxon.
c Wilfred Smith, M.A.Oxon.
W. J. Smith, M.A.Cantab.
c W. L. Snowdon, B.A., Mus.B.Cantab.
a, c J. A. Sowerbutts, M.C., B.Mus.Lond.
b, c John Stainer, B.A., Mus.B.Cantab.
c Heathcote D. Statham, Mus.D.Cantab.
Jack Steadman
a, c Paul Steinitz, D.Mus.Lond.
John Sterling
Bernard Stevens, M.A., Mus.B.Cantab.
Bruce Hylton Stewart, M.A.Cantab.
Pauline Stuart
b, c Harry Stubbs
b, c H. W. Sumsion, C.B.E., D.Mus.Cantuar., B.Mus.Dunelm.
c Alwyn Surplice, B.Mus.Dunelm.
b Geoffrey Tankard
c John A. Tatam, B.Mus.Lond.
Colin Taylor
b E. Kendall Taylor
Eric Taylor, M.A., D.Mus.Oxon.
c Arthur E. Temple, B.Mus.Dunelm.
c Eric H. Thiman, D.Mus.Lond.
R. Harold Thomson, B.Mus.Edin.
c G. H. Thorne, M.A., Mus.B.Cantab.
a Egerton Tidmarsh
c Philip B. Tomblings
Joan Trimble, B.A., Mus.B.Dublin.
J. Clifford Turner
c F. W. Wadely, O.B.E., M.A., Mus.D.Cantab.
c Frederic Waine, M.A., B.Mus.Oxon.
Guy Warrack, B.A., B.Mus.Oxon.
Joyce Warrack
b, c Sydney Watson, M.A., D.Mus.Oxon.
c W. S. Lloyd Webber, D.Mus.Lond.
Yvonne Wells
Philip Wilkinson, D.Mus.Lond., M.Mus.R.C.M.
Denis Williams
c John Williams, M.A., Mus.B.Cantab.
d John Wills
Eric Wilson, M.A., M.Ed.Leeds, D.Mus.Edin.
b Henry Wilson
c John W. Wilson, M.A., Mus.B.Cantab.
a Madeleine Windsor
Herbert Wiseman, M.A.Aberdeen, D.Mus.Edin., F.E.I.S.
Joyce Wodeman
a Robin Wood
R. P. Wood, M.A., Mus.B.Cantab.
c Ronald Woodham, B.A., D.Mus.Oxon.
Victor Yates, M.A., B.Mus.Oxon.
Alexander Youngman, M.A., B.Mus.Oxon

a Fellow of the Royal Academy of Music
b Fellow of the Royal College of Music
c Fellow of the Royal College of Organists
d Fellow of the Royal Manchester College of Music

The Board reserves to itself the right to vary the list of Examiners

Centres and Honorary Local Representatives

ABERDEEN	The Very Rev. Provost W. P. SHANNON, Cathedral House, 4 Rubislaw Den North. Tel.: 36984
ABERYSTWYTH	WILLIAM LEWIS, Esq., University College of Wales. Tel.: 2346/7
AYR	Mrs. CONNELL, L.R.A.M., Belleisle Hotel. Tel.: Alloway 205

*ABERAYRON, ALNWICK, AMERSHAM, ANDOVER, ARMAGH, ASHFORD (KENT), AYLESBURY

BANBURY	Mrs. PHILIP JONES, 26 Dashwood Road. Tel.: 2994
BANGOR (N. WALES) ..	Mrs. EMILIE de R. CLARKE, 1 Bodlondeb, Menai Bridge Road. Tel.: 2460
BARNSTAPLE	Mrs. SIMPSON, Hillworth, 3 Ebberly Lawn. Tel.: 2684
BARROW-IN-FURNESS ..	W. G. BATE, Esq., B.SC., Chief Education Officer, Education Offices. Tel.: 458
BATH	A. W. CLARK, Esq., c/o C. Milsom & Son, North Gate. Tel.: 5675
BELFAST	JOHN H. GRUMMITT, Esq., M.A., Clovelly, Sea Park, Holywood, Belfast. Tel.: Holywood 2434
BERWICK-ON-TWEED ..	Miss DORIS M. DODDS, Murton Mead, 21 Castle Drive. Tel.: 7509
BIRMINGHAM	
	Syllabuses and entry forms can be obtained from The Birmingham School of Music Office, Ratcliffe Place, Birmingham 1
BISHOP AUCKLAND ..	Mrs. ELLEN MAUGHAN, Lightfoot Institute, Kingsway. Tel.: 610
BLACKBURN	W. H. NUTTALL, Esq., 27/31 Penny Street. Tel.: 7314
BLACKPOOL	H. C. LIGHTEN, Esq., F.C.W.A., 696 Devonshire Road, Bispham. Tel.: North Shore 51954
BOGNOR REGIS	Miss WAVENEY GORTON, 4 Shelley Road, Bognor Regis
BOURNEMOUTH	S. G. WEBB, Esq., Minns of Bournemouth, Ltd., 68 Poole Road, Bournemouth West. Tel.: Westbourne 64370
BRADFORD	Miss DOROTHY TANKARD, 15 Wheatlands Drive, Heaton, Bradford, 9. Tel.: Bradford 45634
BRENTWOOD	
BRIDGEND	Mrs. JARVIS, Summerhill School, 66 Park Street. Tel.: 2714
BRIDGWATER	ROBERT H. HAWKINS, Esq., M.ED., B.A., Divisional Education Officer, 11A Cornhill. Tel.: 3064/5
BRIGHTON	Mrs. HELENA THOMAS, 19 Court Ord Road, Rottingdean
BRISTOL	Miss THERESA M. BABBAGE, L.R.A.M., A.R.C.M., 9 Redland Park, Bristol 6. Tel.: 34574
BURNLEY	H. RIDEHALGH, Esq., Arncliffe, Accrington Road, Portfield Bar, Whalley, Nr. Blackburn. Tel.: Whalley 2153
BURTON UPON TRENT ..	Mrs. F. M. HARTSHORN, The Firs, Lower Flat, 45 Rosliston Road, Stapenhill. Tel.: 3249
BURY ST. EDMUNDS ..	Mrs. AUSTIN T. WHITMORE, North End House, 3 Fornham Road. Tel.: 965
BUXTON	GLYNNE D. JONES, Esq., Town Clerk, Town Hall. Tel.: 2060

*BANFF, BARNSLEY, BASINGSTOKE, BATHGATE, BEACONSFIELD, BEDFORD, BIDEFORD, BISHOPS STORTFORD, BLAENAU FFESTINIOG, BLANDFORD, BOLTON, BOSTON, BRIDLINGTON, BRISTOL, BUCKINGHAM, BUDE, BURY (LANCS.)

CAMBRIDGE	G. M. MACFARLANE-GRIEVE, Esq., M.A., Toft Manor. Tel.: Comberton 233
CANTERBURY	LESLIE J. GOULDEN, Esq., c/o Goulden's Music Shop, 36 High Street. Tel.: 4034
CARDIFF	Mrs. E. I. SEATON, 28A Park Road, Whitchurch. Tel.: Cardiff 66032
CARLISLE	Mrs. H. M. PICKLES, B.A., 5 Strand Road. Tel.: 21761
CARMARTHEN	JOHN O. MORGAN, Esq., 25 King Street. Tel.: 6541
CHATHAM	JOHN H. SEARS, Esq., B.A., 242 City Way, Rochester. Tel.: Chatham 43486

CHELMSFORD	
CHELTENHAM	Mrs. JOHN JEENS, A.R.C.M., Kemerton, 35 Tivoli Road. Tel.: 22676
CHESTER	Mrs. C. HODKINSON, 3 Abbey Square. Tel.: 20169
CHESTERFIELD	Mrs. F. J. MILWARD, Aston End, Coal Aston, near Sheffield. Tel.: Dronfield 2241
CHICHESTER	Miss WAVENEY GORTON, 4 Shelley Road, Bognor Regis
CLACTON-ON-SEA ..	Miss CHRISTINE BOND, 10 Worcester Court. Tel.: 1896
COLCHESTER	W. J. HUGHES, Esq., M.A., Scheregate Hotel. Tel.: 73034
CORK	H. FITZGERALD SMITH, Esq., M.R.I.A.I., 73 South Mall. Tel.: 20633

*CARDIGAN, CHESHAM, CIRENCESTER, COLWYN BAY, COVENTRY, CREWE

DARLINGTON	MICHAEL LUCAS, Esq., B.A., 27 Ravensdale Road. Tel.: 66677
DERBY	Miss WINIFRED A. MUNNS, Walkelyne, 14 Rydal Close, Allestree. Tel.: 50825
DONCASTER	Mrs. M. A. WHITE, 9 Lawn Road. Tel.: 3179
DORCHESTER	C. N. GOODMAN, Esq., M.A., South Close, Charminster
DORKING	Miss M. M. CULLEN, M.B.E., Northacre, Westcott, Near Dorking. Tel.: Westcott 89
DOVER	ERIC W. PINNOCK, Esq., 5 Cannon Street. Tel.: 225
DUBLIN	Mrs. OLIVE McHUGH, 10 Rathfarnham Park. Tel.: 906588
DUMFRIES	Miss J. M. DONNAN, Laurel Bank, Laurieknowe. Tel.: 4369
DUNDEE	DAVID L. LAIRD, Esq., c/o Larg & Sons (Dundee) Ltd., 16-24 Whitehall Street. Tel.: 26061
DURHAM	Mrs. C. K. BARRETT, 8 Princes Street, Durham City

*DARTFORD, DEVIZES, DUDLEY, DUNFERMLINE, DUNOON

EASTBOURNE	F. W. A. UPPINGTON, Esq., A.R.C.O.(CHM), 22 Cobbold Avenue. Tel : 4530
EDINBURGH	Mrs. J. W. HOGBEN, 10 Midmar Drive, Edinburgh 10. Tel.: Morningside 1950
ELGIN	Mrs. PHYLLIS F. KNIGHT, Greenhow, Forteath Avenue. Tel.: 7291
EXETER	DENIS J. REED, Esq., Chesterton, 70 Queen's Road. Tel.: 55545

*EAST GRINSTEAD

FALMOUTH	Miss K. V. WORTH, A.R.C.M. Truvady, 34 Tredova Crescent. Tel.: 340
FOLKESTONE	Miss SHEILA MAIN, 6 Ingles Road. Tel.: 51519

*FALKIRK, FISHGUARD

GLASGOW	ROYAL SCOTTISH ACADEMY OF MUSIC, St. George's Place, Glasgow, C.2. Tel.: Douglas 4101
GLOUCESTER	Mrs. JOAN HARRIS, The Garden House, 62A Elmbridge Road. Tel.: 20459
GODALMING	Miss S. D. F. RADCLIFFE, Riverdale. Tel.: Godalming 437
GREENOCK	R. J. ERSKINE ORR, Esq., O.B.E., 14 Charles Street. Tel.: 23301
GRIMSBY	Miss DOROTHY A. TAYLOR, 45 Bargate
GUERNSEY	Mrs. E. N. SCULLY, L.R.A.M., A.R.C.M., 46 Mount Row, St. Peter Port. Tel.: Central 2681

*GAINSBOROUGH, GRAVESEND, GUILDFORD

* Reference should be made to the Central Office.

HALIFAX	Miss ALICE HARWOOD, Rock Leigh, Kensington Road. Tel.: 60300
HARROGATE	GORDON W. G. CASS, Esq., B.SC., A.R.C.M., F.R.G.S., Norwood College. Tel.: 5802
HEREFORD	Mrs. RICHARDSON, Aylestone Hill House, Aylestone Hill. Tel.: 2705
HUDDERSFIELD	SIDNEY H. CROWTHER, Esq., 86 Birkby Hall Road. Tel.: 3123
HULL	GORDON J. RUSSELL, Esq., 13/14 Savile Street. Tel.: Central 35905/6

*HASTINGS, HAVERFORDWEST, HAYWARDS HEATH, HERTFORD, HIGH WYCOMBE, HITCHIN, HORSHAM, HUNTINGDON

INVERNESS	FRANK CRITCHLEY, Esq., 35 Queensgate. Tel.: 32081/2
IPSWICH	SUFFOLK RURAL MUSIC SCHOOL, 8 Soane Street. Tel.: 53426
ISLE OF MAN	HENRY C. WILKINSON, Esq., M.A., Director of Education, Education Office, Strand Street, Douglas. Tel.: 1074
ISLE OF WIGHT	GEORGE F. MEW, Esq., 69 Union Street, Ryde. Tel.: Ryde 2316

*ILFRACOMBE

JERSEY	Mrs. BERYL B. FAIRLIE, L.R.A.M., 15 Netherby Court, Beaumont. Tel.: Southern 438

KENDAL	Miss M. L. WILKINSON, c/o Wilkinson, Sons & Co., Ltd., Organ Works, Aynam Road. Tel.: 262
KETTERING	H. DOUGLAS BILLSON, Esq., Rosedene, Trafalgar Road. Tel.: 2194
KING'S LYNN	GEORGE H. BOTTOMLEY, Esq., M.SC., F.R.I.C., The County Technical College. Tel.: 3425/6/7
KIRKCALDY	R. ALAN NEILL, Esq., Abbotshall Hotel. Tel.: 2803

*KESWICK, KIDDERMINSTER, KILMARNOCK

LANCASTER	E. ARNOLD DOWBIGGIN, Esq., Farringford, Westbourne Road. Tel.: 2113
LEAMINGTON SPA ..	Mrs. FLORENCE M. ASTLEY, A.R.C.M., Brampton, 88 Lillington Road. Tel.: 352
LEEDS	JAMES CHALMERS PARK, Esq., M.C., T.D., 12 Grove Lane, Leeds, 6. Tel.: 53056
LEICESTER	A. RAYMOND WINTER, Esq., c/o Clarke & Satchell Ltd., 8 Hotel Street. Tel.: 58915 (Business); 38669 (Home)
LINCOLN	GEOFFREY A. CHURCH, Esq., B.SC., A.C.G.I., M.I.MECH.E., Technical College, Cathedral Street. Tel.: 24416
LIVERPOOL	ANDREW G. H. RUSHWORTH, Esq., Rushworth & Dreaper, Ltd., 42-46 Whitechapel, Liverpool, 1. Tel.: Royal 9071. Teleg.: Apollo, Liverpool
LONDON AREA	See page 11
LONDONDERRY	WILLIAM A. FRANKLAND, Esq., 33 Marlboro' Street. Tel.: 2131
LOWESTOFT	Mrs. CORKHILL, Injebreck, 94 Cotmer Road, Oulton Broad
LUTON	JOHN E. THOMPSON, Esq., 15/17 Upper George Street. Tel.: 7374

*LAUNCESTON, LITTLEHAMPTON, LLANDRINDOD WELLS, LLANDEILO, LLANELLY, LOUTH, LYME REGIS

Maidstone	ALBERT F. TILLEY, Esq., 454 Loose Road. Tel.: 83222
Malvern, Great ..	Mrs. M. SHARP, 18 Pickersleigh Avenue, Malvern Link. Tel.: Malvern 1304
Manchester	ROYAL MANCHESTER COLLEGE OF MUSIC, Devas Street, Oxford Road, Manchester 15. Tel.: ARDwick 3735
Margate	Mrs. F. CECIL COBB, J.P., Berkeley Lodge, 81 Trinity Square. Tel.: Thanet 20057
Middlesbrough ..	E. D. MASON, Esq., M.A., L.R.A.M., Director of Education, Education Offices, Woodlands Road. Tel.: 46321

*Mansfield, March, Matlock, Merthyr Tydvil, Morpeth

Newcastle-upon-Tyne	E. CROSSLEY FAIRLEY, Esq., 8 Benwell Grove, Newcastle-upon-Tyne, 4. Tel.: 35474
New Milton	Miss C. M. LOVELESS, The Wilderness, Kennard Road. Tel.: 946
Newport (Mon.) ..	JOHN M. SUTTON, Esq., F.I.G.C.M., 112 Cae-Perllan Road. Tel.: 62683
Northampton	PERCY F. GRIFFIN, Esq., 6 Cowper Street. Tel.: 36832
Norwich	S. T. TWEMLOW, Esq., B.MUS., L.R.A.M., County Education Office, Stracey Road, Norwich, NOR 49A. Tel.: 22288
Nottingham	A. H. ATKINSON, Esq., 201 Musters Road, West Bridgford. Tel.: 85014

*Newark, Newbury, Newtown (Mont.), Nuneaton

Oldham	Mrs. T. SUTCLIFFE, 4 Heights Lane, Healds Green, Chadderton
Oxford	LOUIS B. FREWER, Esq., M.A., Tal-y-fan, 58 Sunderland Avenue. Tel.: (Office) 55762; (Home) 56292

*Oswestry

Penzance	Mrs. DONALD BEHENNA, 37 Chapel Street
Perth	IAN McLEISH, Esq., The Music Shop, 41-42 St. John's Square. Tel.: 21818
Peterborough	Mrs. MARTIN PAYNE, St. Andrews, Sawtry, Huntingdon Tel.: Sawtry 371
Plymouth	Miss CECILIA NELDER, Woodcroft, Higher Churchway, Plymstock. Tel.: Plymouth 42324
Pontypridd	D. W. JONES, Esq., Y.M.C.A., Taff Street. Tel.: 2541
Portsmouth	ROBERT W. BRAY, Esq., B.E.M., 25 Elizabeth Gardens, Spencer Road, Southsea
Preston	Miss J. P. GARRATT, 181 Garstang Road, Fulwood. Tel.: 79006

*Penryndeudraeth, Peterhead, Petersfield, Port Talbot, Pwllheli

* Reference should be made to the Central Office.

Reading .. .. .. Mrs. C. D. SMITH,
c/o Metalcraft (Reading) Ltd., 42 South Street. Tel.: 54034

Rhyl .. .. .. Mrs. SHELLEY, East Lodge, Marine Drive. Tel.: 1445

Rochester .. .. JOHN H. SEARS, Esq., B.A.,
242 City Way, Rochester. Tel.: Chatham 43486

Rugby .. .. .. Mrs. S. F. THORPE, Ashbourne Close, 176 Dunchurch Road. Tel.: 3138

*Retford, Rotherham

St. Austell .. .. Mrs. PERRY MORGAN,
Four-Winds, Carlyon Bay, St. Austell. Tel.: Par 2167

Salisbury .. .. P. H. C. CAVENAUGH, Esq., 30a The Close

Sevenoaks .. .. Miss KATHLEEN M. JUDD,
The White Lodge, Hitchen Hatch Lane. Tel.: 53330

Sheffield .. .. T. H. TUNN, Esq., M.A., Director of Education,
Education Office, Leopold Street, Sheffield, 1. Tel.: 26341

Shrewsbury .. .. L. B. DALEY, Esq., M.A., B.SC., M.B.I.M., F.C.C.S.,
Technical College, London Road. Tel.: 51544

Skipton .. .. ..

Southampton .. Miss VIOLET M. BEACH, A.R.C.M.,
83 Highfield Lane, Portswood. Tel. 54823

Southend-on-Sea .. R. G. COMBER, Esq.,
37 Cossington Road, Westcliff-on-Sea. Tel.: Southend 43875

Southport .. ..

Stirling .. .. .. ADAM R. LENNOX, Esq., 14 Melville Terrace. Tel.: 2847

Sunderland .. .. Mrs. C. HARTLEY, 2 Thornhill Gardens. Tel.: 4960

Swansea .. .. .. Mrs. T. S. QUICK, A.R.C.M.,
4 Richmond Road, Cwmdonkin Drive, Uplands. Tel.: 56885

*St. Albans, St. Andrews, St. Ives (Hunts.), Scarborough, Scunthorpe, Seaford, Sheringham, Sidmouth, Skegness, Slough, Solihull, Spalding, Stafford, Stamford, Stockport, Stockton, Stoke-on-Trent, Stourbridge, Stranraer, Stratford-on-Avon, Stroud, Sutton Coldfield, Swindon

Tain .. .. .. W. H. CORMACK, Esq., M.A., LL.B., No. 1 Tower Street. Tel.: 46

Taunton .. .. Mrs. MURIEL G. VAUGHAN, 30 Stoke Road. Tel.: 5725

Tenby .. .. .. WILFRED HARRISON, Esq., M.A., 2 St. Catherine's Terrace

Torquay .. .. Miss E. M. BARTLETT, 63 Audley Avenue. Tel.: 88058

Truro .. .. .. Miss K. V. WORTH, A.R.C.M.,
Truvady, 34 Tredova Crescent, Falmouth. Tel.: Falmouth 340

Tunbridge Wells .. Mrs. W. J. BERRY. St. John's Vicarage, Amherst Road. Tel.: 21183

*Tavistock, Thurso, Tiverton, Tredegar

WAKEFIELD	Mrs. E. EAST, L.R.A.M., 25 Northfield Lane, Horbury, Near Wakefield. Tel.: Horbury 62
WATERFORD	W. G. GOUGH, Esq., 93 Quay. Tel.: 4320
WESTON-SUPER-MARE ..	H. E. COUCH, Esq., 18 Clarence Road South. Tel.: 6509
WEYMOUTH	Mrs. M. HAKES, L.R.A.M., 86 Clearmount Road. Tel.: 1385
WIGAN	ARTHUR HARRIS, Esq., 12 College Road, Upholland. Tel.: Upholland 65
WINCHESTER	Mrs. ALAN RANNIE, West Hayes Lodge, Sarum Road. Tel.: 4364
WOLVERHAMPTON ..	GERALD DE GRAAF, Esq., 20 Cranmore Road. Tel.: 26523
WORCESTER	VICTOR DOWSE, Esq., 1 College Yard. Tel.: 23523
WREXHAM	ARTHUR G. CAMP, Esq., O.B.E., Clarence Villa, 130 Ruabon Road. Tel.: 2531

*WELLS, WELSHPOOL, WELWYN GARDEN CITY, WEST HARTLEPOOL, WHITBY, WHITEHAVEN, WISBECH, WOKING, WORKSOP, WORTHING

YARMOUTH, GREAT ..	C. F. H. CRAWSHAW, Esq., B.A., 11 Queen Street. Tel.: 3454
YEOVIL	Mrs. MARSH-PATTINSON, 4 Penn Hill. Tel.: 76
YORK	Miss THEO CARCAUD, 3A Minster Court

LONDON AREA

*ROYAL ACADEMY OF MUSIC	York Gate, Marylebone Road, N.W.1
*ROYAL COLLEGE OF MUSIC	Prince Consort Road, South Kensington, S.W.7
BLACKHEATH	NOEL FUSSELL, Esq., 4 Duke Humphrey Road, S.E.3. Tel.: LEE 2506
BROMLEY	H. H. CHAPPLE, Esq., 21 Aldermary Road. Tel.: RAV. 7364
CROYDON	Mrs. H. CARRICK SMITH, The Homestead, Coombe Lane. Tel.: Addiscombe 4049
EALING	Mrs. YVONNE FRANKLIN, A.R.C.M., 58 Clitherow Avenue, Hanwell, W.7. Tel.: GEO 4921.
HARROW	Miss MARGARET I R. WALLACE, Roselyon, Mount Park Road. Tel.: Byron 1252
KINGSTON-UPON-THAMES	Mrs. MANNING, 50 Latchmere Road. Tel.: KIN. 6428
WATFORD	T. RIGBY TAYLOR, Esq., C.B.E., J.P., Ashlands, Stratford Road. Tel.: 24389
WIMBLEDON	Mrs. VOKES, 77 Coombe Lane, S.W.20. Tel.: WIM. 4578

*BARNET, CHINGFORD, CROUCH END, EDGWARE, ENFIELD, EPSOM, FINCHLEY, ILFORD, REDHILL, ROMFORD, STREATHAM, SUTTON, TOTTENHAM, UXBRIDGE, WALTHAMSTOW, WEMBLEY, WOODFORD

---

* Reference should be made to the Central Office.
Additional Centres will be arranged in other towns as necessity arises.
For places of Examination, see Regulation 4.

GENERAL REGULATIONS

FOR THE YEAR JANUARY-DECEMBER 1964

---

1. Grades of Examination

Grade I (Primary)	Grade V (Higher)
Grade II (Elementary)	Grade VI (Intermediate)
Grade III (Transitional)	Grade VII (Advanced)
Grade IV (Lower)	Grade VIII (Final)

Candidates may be entered in any Grade irrespective of age, and without previously having taken any other Grade in the same subject.

Candidates for Practical Grades VI, VII and VIII must already have passed the Board's examination in Theory Grade V before the last date of entry for the Practical, i.e., in some previous period. There is no compulsory Written work for Practical Grades I to V.

Exemption from Theory Grade V may be claimed on the entry form for Practical examinations by candidates:—

(*a*) who have passed Theory Grade VI, VII or VIII;

(*b*) who have passed in Music as a subject for the General Certificate of Education of one of the examining bodies listed on page 86;

(*c*) who wish to enter for a Practical examination in Grade VI or VII solely for the purpose of fulfilling the Advanced Level requirements of one of the G.C.E. examining bodies—see page 86. (In this case the result is sent direct to the G.C.E. authority, no mark form or certificate being issued by the Board.)

2. Subjects

I. Written Examinations

Theory of Music.

II. Practical Examinations

Pianoforte, Pianoforte Duets, Organ, Violin, Viola, Violoncello, Double Bass, Singing, Harp, Wind Instruments, General Musicianship.

III. Inspections and Classes

General Inspection and Report, Chamber Music for Instrumental Ensembles, Class Singing.

3. Dates of Examinations, 1964

WRITTEN

Period A	..	**Saturday, 29th February (2 p.m.)**
Period B	..	**Wednesday, 17th June (5 p.m.)**
Period C	..	**Thursday, 5th November (2 p.m.)**

Candidates should be entered only in the Period in which the appointed day and time is suitable, as in no circumstances can they be examined on any other date.

PRACTICAL

*Period A	..	**2nd March to 26th March and 31st March to 4th April,** in the London area also on **11th April**
Period B	..	**25th May to 6th June,** in Ireland† **25th May to 27th June,** in Scotland **22nd June to 18th July,** in England and Wales, in the London area also on **25th July**
Period C	..	**16th November to 12th December** (continuing to **19th December** in the London area)

Appointments for Practical examinations can be fixed by the Board only after the entries are complete and the Examiners' circuits arranged.

Space is given on the entry forms for applicants to state:—

(*a*) dates or times not convenient;

(*b*) preferences for days of the week or times of day (not for a specific date).

Schools must declare on the entry form any dates in the school calendar on which examination would be specially inconvenient, and should state the last day of term.

The Board will do its utmost to avoid dates inconvenient to candidates if so declared at the time of entry; but, having regard to the numerous schools and candidates for whom arrangements have to be made, it cannot give a prior undertaking to examine on or to avoid a particular date and must reserve the right to plan the Examiners' circuits in a manner best suited to the majority.

Private teachers may, if necessary, state a preference for appointments out of school or working hours and the earliest and latest hours of day at which candidates who have to travel a distance to a Centre can conveniently attend. Appointments would not normally be given before 9 a.m. or after 6.30 p.m.

Reference should be made to Regulation 9 on page 15.

---

* In Scotland, Practical examinations will not be held in Period A in Ross and Cromarty, Sutherland and Caithness. Teachers in this area are asked to concentrate their entries in the June—July and the November—December periods.

† Examinations for the Diploma L.R.S.M. will also be held (in Dublin only).

4. Place of Examination

The Examinations will ordinarily be held at:—

(*a*) Local Centres named on pages 6-11 in accommodation arranged by the Board in accordance with the number and distribution of the entries.

(*b*) Schools approved by the Board.

See Regulations 17 and 20.

The Board reserves the right to summon candidates if necessary to attend at some central place as near to their schools or homes as can be arranged. For the Practical examinations, however, arrangements can usually be made for an Examiner to visit a school, subject to Regulation 20, paragraphs (*b*) and (*c*) (page 24).

5. Method of Entry for Examination

Candidates should be entered by a school or by a teacher of music or by a parent or guardian. Adult students may enter themselves. Proper entry forms must be used.

Each form contains space for the names of ten candidates in any Grades; there is one form for Practical entries and another for Theory.

Applications for entry forms should be made not less than one week before the last day of entry, preferably by postcard.

6. Examination Fees, 1964

	Theory		Practical		
	s.	d.	£	s.	d.
Grade I (Primary)	12	0	1	0	0
Grade II (Elementary) ..	13	0	1	1	0
Grade III (Transitional) ..	14	0	1	3	0
Grade IV (Lower)	15	0	1	5	0
Grade V (Higher)	16	0	1	7	0
Grade VI (Intermediate) ..	18	0	1	10	0
Grade VII (Advanced) ..	19	0	2	0	0
Grade VIII (Final)	20	0	2	10	0

Division—	Junior			Middle			Senior		
	£	s.	d.	£	s.	d.	£	s.	d.
Pianoforte Duets (per pair)	1	8	0	1	10	0	1	12	0

The full fee is required for re-entry. An official receipt will be posted from the Board's office to the person who signs the entry form.

7. Dates of Entry for Examination, 1964

Entry forms, together with the full fees, must reach 14 Bedford Square, London, W.C.1 on or before the following dates:

For March—April	..	**22nd January**
For June—July	..	**22nd April** from Scotland (and Berwick) and Ireland
" " "	..	**13th May** from England and Wales
For Nov.—Dec.	..	**30th September**

No entries will be accepted after these dates, either at the ordinary fees or upon payment of an extra fee.

8. Acceptance of Entry

Entries for examination can be accepted by the Board only in accordance with the conditions and regulations contained in this syllabus, and on the understanding that in all matters the decision of the Board must be accepted as final.

A candidate may enter for only one grade of Theory at a time.

The Board reserves the right to refuse or cancel the entry of any candidate, in which case the examination fee will be returned.

The Board reserves the right to invalidate the examination of any candidate entered incorrectly. Care must be taken to enter candidates' full names on the entry forms.

9. Notices of Date and Time of Examination

Notices, stating the precise time, date and place, either for an Examiner to visit a school or for the candidates to attend at a local centre, will be sent as early as possible to the persons who have signed the entry forms.

The Board requires all candidates to be present for examination accordingly, and cannot undertake to alter the appointments when once the notices have been issued.

10. Absence

(*a*) **Notice of withdrawal** of any candidate who cannot be present for examination must be sent in writing direct to the Secretary at 14 Bedford Square, London, W.C.1 (or by telegram to Musexam Westcent London) *immediately the inability is known.* A medical certificate is not required.

Candidates in quarantine for any infection must be withdrawn. If the visit of an Examiner to a school has to be cancelled because the whole school has been placed in quarantine, special arrangements for deferment or for a concession in respect of the fees may be made by the Board at its discretion.

The names of candidates withdrawn or absent without notice cannot be carried forward in the Board's office to a later period, but may be entered again in the normal way (Regulations 5 and 6).

(*b*) **Refund of fees.** The Board gives no undertaking to return entry fees, or any portion of them. Any refund which may be made is entirely at the discretion of the Board.

Provided notice of withdrawal has been given as required in (*a*) the Board will, in the normal course, make a refund on a fixed scale approximating to three-quarters of the fee if the notice is received within 15 days of the date on which entries closed, and approximating to half the fee if the notice is received more than 15 days after that date, but is sent not later than the day of the examination.

Notice of withdrawal given only to an Examiner, Honorary Local Representative, steward or invigilator at the examination centre, instead of to the Board's office in London, is not enough to qualify for a refund.

11. Results of Examination

The Examiners report to the Board and are not allowed to give any information as to the results of examination to any other person or persons.

As soon as possible after the Practical examination the Board will send by post to the person by whom the entry form was signed a detailed mark form, of which there is no duplicate, showing the number of marks awarded to each candidate and the Examiner's remarks; for the Theory examinations only the total of marks will be stated.

The Board does not accept responsibility for the non-receipt of any mark form after its despatch by post. Results of the Practical examinations will be sent by registered post if request is made by remittance of the postal registration fee with the examination fees.

On application and the payment of a fee of 2s. 6d. the total of the marks obtained by a candidate, but not the details, may be repeated.

12. Allotment of Marks

In the Practical examinations out of a possible 150 marks, 100 are required to Pass, 120 to Pass with Merit, and 130 for Distinction.

The standard of the examination is set by the Pass marks, and Examiners add or deduct marks therefrom. Marks are not awarded either by deduction from the maximum or by addition from zero.

In the Theory of Music examinations 66 marks are required to Pass, out of a possible 99; in Grades I to V there are no classifications of Merit or Distinction; in Grades VI to VIII candidates gaining 90 marks or more will be classified as having passed with Distinction.

13. Certificates

Certificates will be awarded to successful candidates, and will specify the subject and the Grade in which they have been examined.

These certificates will not certify that the holders thereof are qualified to teach, nor entitle them to append any letters to their names.

A duplicate of a certificate lost or destroyed can usually be provided on payment of a search fee of 5s. The Board cannot be responsible for the loss of certificates in the post.

14. Special Certificates

The Board will grant a special certificate to any candidate who has passed the four highest Grades in succession, e.g. Grades V, VI, VII and VIII in that order, in the same subject.

Application for this certificate must be made on a form which can be obtained from the Central Office. The Board reserves the right to require the production of the certificate of any Grade for verification; all certificates thus forwarded will be returned.

SCHOLARSHIPS, MEDALS AND PRIZES

15. Scholarships (see page 87)

The following were elected to scholarships in May 1963:—

Rosalind J. Bevan, Potters Bar (Pianoforte)
Joan F. Clamp, Swadlincote (Oboe)
Douglas J. Cummings, London (Violoncello)
Nina E. Martin, London (Violin)
Bryn J. P. Turley, Cambridge (Pianoforte)
Anthony P. Winter, London (Clarinet)

16. Medallists

In each Period of the examinations in each of Grades VI, VII and VIII the candidates who obtain the highest and second highest Distinction marks of not less than 135 in a Practical subject are Gold and Silver Medallists respectively and receive presentation volumes of their own choice.

No candidate can take more than one of these awards in the same Grade and subject.

The following were declared Medallists as a result of the examinations held in 1962:

	GOLD MEDALLISTS
Grade VIII (Final)	Alison Chamberlain, Northampton Joan F. Clamp, Leicester Jon C. Earnshaw, Leeds Jane Hyland, Portsmouth Danielle J. Salamon, Leeds Rosemary Wilton, Newcastle-under-Lyme
Grade VII (Advanced)	Lionel Friend, High Wycombe Martin V. Jones, Coventry Jeanne Smith, Bournemouth Tan Oon Choo, Sevenoaks
Grade VI (Intermediate)	John G. Hobbs, Birmingham Margaret Holden, Fulwood Robert Stoodley, Yeovil
	SILVER MEDALLISTS
Grade VIII (Final)	John Falconer, Edinburgh David L. Humphreys, Cambridge Richard Hutt, Jersey Bryn J. P. Turley, Rochester Richard B. Weigall, Lyme Regis
Grade VII (Advanced)	Deborah J. Bryde, Bebington Paul Inwood, Wimbledon Jane Leese, Leeds Susan Martin, Oxford Alan Wilson, Nottingham
Grade VI (Intermediate)	M. Jean Alcock, Liverpool Margaret J. Dorée, Blackheath Mary Faulkner, Orpington Lindy J. Rutter, Farnham (Surrey) David Soutar, Ayr Michael Young, Wolverhampton

16a. Local Prizes

The annual prizes for which the Board has been entrusted with capital funds or endowments were awarded for 1962 as follows:

BLACKBURN. *Frances E. Walker Memorial Prize for Grade VII*

Pianoforte	Valerie A. Knowles

BOURNEMOUTH AND NEW MILTON. *Edie Marr Prize for Grade VI*

Pianoforte	Nigel Boylin

CARSHALTON MUSIC PRIZE *for Grade VI, VII or VIII*

Grade VI Pianoforte	Angela East

DUNDEE. *Nora C. Leggatt Prizes for Pianoforte*

Grade VI	Norma Low
Grade VII	Joy Drury Brian M. Hirst

GLASGOW. *Nivena Macduff Prizes for Pianoforte*

Grade I	Beth McConochie
Grade II	Paul C. G. McGlone
Grade III	Frances M. Fitzpatrick
Grade IV	Leslie J. Eddleston Margaret McK. Parker

LEEDS AND HARROGATE. *Lloyd Hartley Memorial Prizes for Pianoforte*

Grade VI for Leeds and Harrogate	Carol A. Clark
Grade VII for Leeds	Jane Leese
Grade VII for Harrogate	Mary E. Davies Jennifer M. Speirs Penelope J. Trees
Grade VIII for Leeds	Danielle Salamon
Grade VIII for Harrogate	Jane M. C. Rae

HUDDERSFIELD. *Elsie Roberts Prize for Pianoforte Grade VI, VII or VIII*

Grade VI	Susan M. Worsley

LANCASTER. *Lloyd Hartley Memorial Prize for Pianoforte*

Grade VIII	Christine White

MANCHESTER. *Sarino and Gladys Besso Memorial Prize for Pianoforte*

Grade V	Ian K. Garner Patricia Moors

NEWCASTLE-ON-TYNE. *Sir William E. Bigge Memorial Prize for Grade VI or VII*

Grade VI Pianoforte	Geoffrey H. Dancer

NORFOLK, COUNTY OF. *Saxton Noble Memorial Prizes for Grades VI and VII*

Grade VI Pianoforte	Anna E. Sutherland
Grade VII Pianoforte	Janet Bowden

PLYMOUTH. *Mrs. Hamilton Akaster Memorial Prize for Strings Grade V or VI*

Grade VI Violin	David N. Matheson

SKIPTON. *Lloyd Hartley Memorial Prize for Pianoforte*

Grade VIII	Vivienne M. Rowe

In Cheltenham and Gloucester, Glasgow, Hertford, and Plymouth, other prizes are provided by the generosity of individual donors, or from local trusts, of which particulars can be had on application to the Central Office.

WRITTEN EXAMINATIONS

17. Conduct of the Written Examinations

(*a*) Examinations will be held in public Centres (see pages 6 to 11) under the supervision of the Honorary Local Representatives or their deputies, or of invigilators appointed by the Board, in all towns from which sufficient entries are received. The most convenient Centre must be specified on the entry form.

(b) Examinations may be held at any School approved by the Board if application is made upon the entry form, and if the Headmaster or Headmistress accepts responsibility for the safe custody of the papers and proper conduct of the examination. The duty of invigilation may be delegated by the Head to a responsible deputy.

(*c*) The invigilator must be present during the whole time of the examination.

(*d*) The invigilator must open the sealed packet of examination papers in the examination room in the presence of the candidates, and inform them:—

that they must work their papers without help and without reference to notes or books of any kind, and that any candidate infringing this rule or helping another will be disqualified;

that they must write their names in full at the top of their papers;

that their answers must be written on the printed question papers;

that they are not allowed to take copies of the papers nor their rough notes from the room;

that the time allowed for working it is printed at the top of each question paper.

In public Centres the Board will provide plain ruled manuscript paper on which candidates may do their rough working; at schools this may be provided by the school. All candidates should bring their own pens or pencils.

(*e*) Time allowed for the working of papers:—

Grades I to V	2 hours
Grades VI to VIII	3 hours

Candidates may hand in their papers at any time after 40 minutes from the start, but having done so must leave the room and may not return. No candidate arriving more than 35 minutes after the start can be admitted.

(*f*) As each paper is handed in the invigilator must see that the candidate's name in full is written legibly at the top of it.

(*g*) The invigilator, before leaving the room, must seal the papers, which must be returned as soon as possible to the Board's Office by registered post, with a signed declaration stating that the examination has been conducted in conformity with these Regulations.

The invigilator must return, with the completed examination papers, any question papers remaining unworked.

(*h*) **Blind Candidates** entering for the written examinations will be supplied with the examination papers in Braille type and the answers will be accepted in Braille, provided application is made at the time of entry. Alternatively, or in addition, arrangements could be made for a blind candidate's answers to be written down by an amanuensis.

18. Past Examination Papers

Copies of the question papers set in the written examinations may be purchased from 1st January of the following year from the Publications Department or through a music-seller.

THEORY

19. Requirements for the Examinations in Theory of Music

(i) The Papers in each Grade will be related generally to the corresponding Grade in the Practical examinations. Questions may vary each Period in type and style, and in number.

(ii) The Syllabus is progressive and cumulative from Grade I upwards. The Examiners will expect candidates to have knowledge of any subjects specified in the preceding Grades. Questions may be asked on terms and signs, and in Grade V onwards on ornaments, such as are commonly found in music set for the corresponding Practical Grade.

(iii) The Board refrains from naming special text books, and the Examiners will accept correct and intelligent answers without reference to particular systems or methods.

Grade I (Primary)

(*a*) The staff. G and F clefs. Names of notes. The sharp, flat and natural. Construction of the major scale; major keys of C, G, D and F, with their key signatures and tonic triads (root position).

(*b*) Time values of notes, dotted notes and rests. Simple time signatures.

(*c*) Terms and signs (in accordance with (ii) above).

Grade II (Elementary)

As in Grade I, with the addition of:—

(*a*) Leger lines. Construction of the minor scale (choice given of melodic or harmonic form). Keys of A major and A, E and D minor, with their signatures and tonic triads, root, in close position. Diatonic intervals in the specified keys (five major and three minor) from the tonic up to the fifth.

(*b*) 6/8 time. Triplets. Barring an unbarred phrase. Rhythm of musical phrases in relation to words.

(*c*) Terms and signs (in accordance with (ii) above).

Grade III (Transitional)

As in Grades I and II, with the addition of:—

(*a*) Major keys of E, B♭, E♭ and A♭; minor keys (choice given of either form of the scale) of G and C; their signatures and tonic triads, root, in close position. Diatonic intervals in the nine specified major keys from the tonic upwards; and in the five specified minor keys from the tonic up to the fifth.

(*b*) As in Grades I and II, with more advanced questions and including any form of compound duple time.

(*c*) Terms and signs (in accordance with (ii) above).

Grade IV (Lower)

As in preceding Grades, with the addition of:—

(*a*) Major keys of B, F♯, D♭ and G♭; minor keys (choice given of either form of the scale) of B, F♯, C♯, F and B♭; their key signatures and tonic triads, root, in close position. Diatonic intervals in the specified keys (minor scales in harmonic form) from the tonic upwards. Transposing a melody from treble to bass and vice versa, at the octave.

(*b*) Simple and compound times with their signatures. Barring an unbarred phrase.

(*c*) Terms and signs (in accordance with (ii) above).

Grade V (Higher)

(*a*) All major and all minor (choice given of either minor form) scales and keys with their signatures. The technical names for the notes of the scale (tonic, dominant, etc.). Intervals and their inversions formed on each degree of the major and harmonic minor scale. Double flats and double sharps. Transposing a simple melody into another key.

(*b*) Simple and compound times with their signatures. Barring of unbarred phrases. Completion of incomplete bars with rests.

(*c*) Terms, signs and ornaments (in accordance with (ii) above).

(*d*) Tonic triads in close position and their inversions in major and minor keys. The three primary chords (I, IV and V) in root position in any key (root, 3rd or 5th at the top, with three notes on the treble staff and one on the bass).

(*e*) Writing a rhythm (on one note) to fit given words; adding an answering phrase to a given phrase.

Grade VI (Intermediate)

(*a*) All major and all harmonic and melodic minor scales and keys with their signatures. The harmonic chromatic scale. Intervals as in Grade V, and compound intervals.

(*b*) As in Grade V with more advanced questions.

(*c*) Terms, signs and ornaments (in accordance with (ii) above).

(*d*) Triads and their inversions on each note of major and minor scales. The three primary chords as in Grade V and also in progressions forming perfect, imperfect and plagal cadences.

(*e*) Writing a melody to given words; adding an answering phrase to complete a given four-bar phrase.

(*f*) Simple questions about established composers and their standard works, and about the instruments of the orchestra. A wide choice will be given.

Grade VII (Advanced)

(*a*) Major, minor and harmonic chromatic scales in all keys. Intervals and triads and their inversions.

(*b*) Terms, signs and ornaments (in accordance with (ii) above).

(*c*) Common chords on the tonic, subdominant, dominant and submediant, laid out as for four voices S.A.T.B., two notes on the treble staff and two on the bass, and also in successions as in the four cadences.

(*d*) Harmonisation in four parts of a simple melody or of an unfigured bass. Construction of a phrase on a given harmonic basis. Knowledge of chords, I, II, IV, V, VI and their inversions, and of the use of unaccented passing-notes, will be expected.

(*e*) Writing a melody to given words; completing a melody of which the beginning is given (the whole melody limited to 12 bars); simple modulations may be required.

(*f*) Adding another melody above or below a given melody.

(*g*) Phrasing and structure of melodies. Simple harmonic analysis.

(*h*) Questions of a general nature about established composers and their standard works, and about the instruments of the orchestra. A wide choice will be given.

Grade VIII (Final)

(*a*) A knowledge of any of the subjects specified in sections (*a*) and (*b*) of the preceding Grades will be expected, with the addition of the C clef for alto or tenor.

(*b*) General knowledge of the common musical forms.

(*c*) Four-part chords formed on all degrees of major and minor scales, first and second inversions, the chord of the dominant seventh and its inversions, modulation to related keys and the simple use of unessential notes, i.e., the use of accented and unaccented passing notes, but not including suspensions. The tests may take the form of harmonisation of a melody in 4 vocal parts or in a simple Pianoforte style, and/or the working of a figured or an unfigured bass.

(*d*) Adding another melody above or below a given melody; writing a melody to given words; completing a melody of which the beginning is given.

(*e*) Analysis of the rhythmic structure of a melody, and phrasing. Analysis of harmonic progressions, including modulations, in a straightforward passage which will not require a greater knowledge of harmony than for (*c*) above.

(*f*) Questions about established composers and their standard works (the identification of the principal themes being one of the alternative questions which might be set) and about the instruments of the orchestra. A wide choice will be given.

PRACTICAL EXAMINATIONS

20. Conduct of Practical Examinations

(*a*) Centres will be arranged where Stewards appointed by the Honorary Local Representatives or by the Board will be in charge outside the rooms in which Examiners will hear candidates. The Board may call on all candidates to attend at a Centre irrespective of the number entered by any one teacher. Consideration will be given to requests as to the place of examination if they are noted on the entry forms; the Board cannot undertake to deal with requests made after the time of entry.

(*b*) Visits of Examiners to boarding or day schools or schools of music where there are 12 or more candidates may, at the Board's discretion, be arranged if requested on the entry form. Under suitable conditions this facility may be extended to teachers' studios. Where a school at which examinations are to take place is some distance from the nearest station, the school or teacher must arrange transport for the Examiner and may send the account to the Board.

(*c*) Schools and Teachers who apply to have Practical examinations on their own premises under (*b*) must provide a suitable room where the tests will not be overheard, quiet, well-lighted and warm, containing a good pianoforte properly regulated and in tune, a writing-table and chair for the Examiner, and someone to act as Steward outside the examination room.

(*d*) There may be one or more Examiners at the option of the Board; no other person will normally be allowed in the room with the candidate (except an accompanist) during the progress of an examination; but if notice is given to the Board at the time of entry the principal of a school or the teacher may appoint someone who is not a teacher of music nor a relative of the candidate to be present.

(*e*) Candidates requiring accompaniment must provide their own accompanist and the teacher may act as such (the Examiner will not); but the accompanist may remain in the room only whilst actually engaged in accompanying. Candidates are recommended to provide themselves with music stands if they require them.

(*f*) Although Examiners may at their discretion take more or less time over the examination of separate candidates, the time to be allowed is as follows:—

Grade I	10 minutes	Grade VI	20 minutes
Grades II and III ..	12 ,,	Grade VII	25 ,,
Grades IV and V ..	15 ,,	Grade VIII ..	30 ,,

Three extra minutes are allowed in Grades I to V for Stringed and Wind instruments.

(*g*) Candidates must be presented in the order on the Door List which will be the same as on the entry form, unless a revised order is given to the Examiner before the first candidate enters.

21. Requirements for Practical Examinations

(*a*) Candidates may use any edition of the music. When any particular edition is quoted in this syllabus it is intended solely as a means of identification and its use is not compulsory. Where there are no printed expression marks, as may happen in some copyright editions, candidates should use discretion to achieve a musical performance.

(*b*) Any candidate offering a *wrong study or piece* or not being prepared to perform the whole of the work specified in the syllabus of the *current year for the Grade under examination will be liable to disqualification.

(*c*) It is not necessary that studies and pieces should be played at the exact speed indicated by any metronome marks.

(*d*) The Examiner may, at his discretion, stop the performance of any particular study or piece at a point when he has heard enough to form his judgment. Candidates should carry out D.C. directions, and should clearly understand "repeat" signs, but "repeats" should not be played in the examination unless the Examiner asks for them.

(*e*) Playing the prepared pieces from memory is optional. Candidates playing from memory must bring copies of the pieces for the Examiner's use.

(*f*) **Blind Candidates.** The Royal National Institute for the Blind transcriptions of the 1964 examination books for Grades I to VI will be in the new style Braille (bar over bar, with the intervals in the right hand reading downwards). In Grades VII and VIII some of the pieces will be in the old style Braille and some in the new. Enquiries regarding this should be addressed to the Royal National Institute for the Blind, 224-9 Great Portland Street, London, W.1.

It must be stated on the entry form that the candidates are blind and that as an alternative to sight reading they will take either reading from Braille or memory (repetition) tests. The reading tests for Pianoforte Grades I to V and for Violin will not be affected by the new Braille notation, but candidates in Pianoforte Grades VI to VIII will be given the option of reading the tests in either the old or the new notation.

Specimens showing the standard of the Braille tests for Pianoforte can be obtained from the Royal National Institute for the Blind.

Memory Test. The candidate will be required to repeat on his instrument (or vocally if entered as a singer) short passages played on the pianoforte by the examiner, who will give the key chord, name the key, and then play the passage three times before asking the candidate to repeat it and to describe the time. The examiner will then play the passage a fourth time, bar by bar, asking the candidate to name the notes and to give their time values. The passages consist in Grades I to V of a single part, in Grade VI of two parts, and in Grades VII and VIII of four-part harmony, all about four bars in length. In the last two grades candidates will be asked to describe the chords or progressions.

---

* In the March/April period only, the pieces set for the previous year may be played —see Notices on page 1.

AURAL TESTS*

included in the practical examination of all subjects

For Test A, and any others which must be "sung", pitch rather than vocal quality is the object. The Examiner will keep within the vocal compass of the candidate, who may sing on "lah" or any vowel sound or may hum. Boys with breaking voices may whistle or may hum an octave lower.

For Test B in Grades I to IV, and in B2 Grade V, candidates may use sol-fa or numbers, and should be ready to tell the Examiner which they prefer.

For Test C, when asked to beat time, candidates should do so by an arm movement from the elbow, down-up for duple, down-right-up for triple, down-left-right-up for quadruple. When asked to clap, they may clap hands or tap with one hand on a hard surface, as they prefer. In C. 1, Grades I to III, and in C, Grades IV to VI, the passages and melodies played by the Examiner will be in simple time.

Candidates will be asked:—

Grade I (Primary)

A. To sing a note between middle C and treble C played by the Examiner.

B. To say whether a note is the 2nd, 3rd, 4th or 5th of a major scale, or to give its sol-fa name, when it has been played by the Examiner after the key-chord and key-note.

C. 1. To say whether a harmonised passage played by the Examiner is in duple or triple time, and to beat time whilst the same music is being played a second time.

2. To clap the rhythm-pattern of a short melody played twice by the Examiner.

Grade II (Elementary)

A. To sing a group of three related notes played twice by the Examiner in a major key. The key-chord will first be sounded.

B. 1. To say whether a note is the 2nd, 3rd, 4th or 5th of a major scale, or to give its sol-fa name, when it has been played by the Examiner after the key-chord and key-note.

2. To sing any of the first five notes of a major scale requested by the Examiner after sounding the key-chord and key-note.

---

* Numerous examples of the tests are given in "Aural Tests" published by the Board in three parts—Part I for Grades I to V, Part II for Grades VI and VII, and Part III for Grade VIII. They are obtainable at 3s. 6d. each from the Publishing Manager or through any music-seller.

Candidates will be asked:—

C. 1. To say whether a melody played by the Examiner is in duple or triple time, and to beat time whilst the same music is being played a second time.

2. To clap the rhythm-pattern of a shorter melody played twice by the Examiner.

Grade III (Transitional)

A. 1. To sing a group of four related notes played twice by the Examiner in a major key. The key-chord will first be sounded.

2. To sing the upper or lower note of a consonant interval played harmonically by the Examiner.

B. To sing any note of a major scale requested by the Examiner, the key-chord and key-note having been sounded.

C. 1. To say whether a melody played by the Examiner is in duple, triple or quadruple time, and to beat time whilst the same music is being played a second time.

2. To clap the rhythm-pattern of a shorter melody played twice by the Examiner.

Grade IV (Lower)

A. 1. To sing a group of five related notes played twice by the Examiner in a major key. The key-chord will first be sounded.

2. To sing the upper or lower note of a consonant interval played harmonically by the Examiner, and to describe the interval as a 3rd, 4th, 5th, 6th or 8th. (It is *not* necessary to state major, minor or perfect.)

B. To sing any note of a major scale requested by the Examiner, the key-chord and key-note having been sounded.

C. To clap the rhythm-pattern of a melody played twice by the Examiner; to say whether the time is duple, triple or quadruple; and to beat time when the music is repeated by the Examiner.

Grade V (Higher)

A. 1. To sing a short melodic phrase played twice by the Examiner the key-chord having been sounded.

2. To sing the highest, middle or lowest note, or all three notes in succession, of a major or minor triad, root position only, sounded harmonically in close position, and to say whether the triad is major or minor.

(*continued*)

Candidates will be asked:—

B. 1. To give the letter-name of any note played by the Examiner in the major scale of C or G or F, within an octave, after he has named and played the key-chord and key-note.

2. To sing any note of a major scale requested by the Examiner, the key-chord and key-note having been sounded. (The letter names will not be used in this test.)

C. To clap the rhythm-pattern of a melody played twice by the Examiner; to say whether the time is duple, triple or quadruple; and to beat time when the music is repeated by the Examiner.

Grade VI (Intermediate)

A. 1. To sing or play from memory the *upper* part of an easy two-part phrase played twice by the Examiner, the key-chord having been sounded.

2. To sing the highest, middle or lowest note, or all three notes in succession, of a major or minor triad sounded harmonically in close position; to describe the triad as major or minor; and to state whether the lowest note played is the root, third or fifth of the chord. Candidates may describe the chord as in root position or first or second inversion.

B. To sing any note of the harmonic minor scale requested by the Examiner immediately after sounding the key-note, which will be at a pitch between B and D inclusive.

C. To clap the rhythm-pattern of a melody played twice by the Examiner; to say whether the time is duple, triple or quadruple; and to beat time when the music is repeated by the Examiner.

D. To recognise cadences in a major key as perfect, plagal, imperfect or interrupted in phrases played twice by the Examiner after the key-chord has been sounded.

Grade VII (Advanced)

A. To sing or play from memory the *lower* part of a two-part phrase in a major key played twice by the Examiner, the key-chord having been sounded.

B. To sing the highest, middle or lowest note of a major or minor triad sounded harmonically in close or open position; to describe the triad as major or minor; and to identify the lowest note played as the root, third or fifth of the chord, or to describe the chord as in root position or first or second inversion; and to identify the highest note played as the root, third or fifth.

Candidates will be asked:—

C. 1. To clap the rhythm-pattern of a melody played twice by the Examiner; to say whether the time is simple or compound duple, triple or quadruple; and to beat time when the music is repeated by the Examiner.

2. To identify note-values (e.g., as minim, crotchet, quaver, including dotted notes) of a short time-pattern in 2/4, 3/4 or 4/4 played twice by the Examiner, who will name the time-signature and signify the speed of the pulse.

D. To recognise cadences in major and minor keys as perfect, plagal, imperfect or interrupted as these occur in a musical sentence played twice by the Examiner, the key-chord having been sounded.

Grade VIII (Final)

A. 1. To sing or play from memory the *lower* part of a two-part phrase in a major or minor key played twice by the Examiner, the key-chord having been sounded.

2. To sing or play from memory a short melodic phrase in a major key played twice by the Examiner. Thereafter to give the letter-name of each note as the phrase, or part of it, is slowly played again by the Examiner, who will first play and name the key-note.

B. To name as tonic or dominant or subdominant, and to define as in root position or first or second inversion, a four-part chord in a major key played by the Examiner after he has played the tonic chord in root position.

C. To clap the rhythm-pattern of a melody played twice by the Examiner; to say whether the time is simple or compound duple, triple or quadruple, and to beat time when the music is repeated by the Examiner. In addition, to identify note-values (e.g., as minim, crotchet, quaver, semiquaver, including dotted notes) of a portion of it played again by the Examiner after he has named the note-value of the beat.

D. 1. To recognise cadences in major and minor keys as perfect, plagal, imperfect or interrupted as these occur in a musical sentence played twice by the Examiner, the key-chord having been sounded.

2. To say whethe- a short passage played once by the Examiner beginning in a major key modulates to its dominant, or subdominant, or relative minor. The tonic chord will first be sounded.

PIANOFORTE

Schedule of maximum marks:—

	Grade	I-V	VI, VII	VIII
Scales		18	24	24
Broken Chords or Arpeggios ..		15		
Studies and Pieces—	1	27	27	27
	2	27	27	36
	3	27	18	27
	4	—	18	—
Playing at Sight		18	18	18
Aural Tests		18	18	18
Total		150	150	150

The Examiners in marking will pay attention not only to accuracy of notes and time, but also to other things inherent in a good performance, for example, quality of touch, variety and gradation of tone, choice of tempo, observance of marks of expression, rhythm, phrasing and accent, and the use of practical fingering.

Scales, arpeggios and broken chords should be played from memory, ascending and descending throughout the prescribed compass, at a *pace appropriate to the technical demands of the grade*, consistent with accuracy and distinctness, and without undue accentuation. In all grades broken chords and arpeggios should be played legato; scales in Grades I to VII legato, but in Grade VIII legato or staccato as directed by the examiner. Any practical and systematic fingering which produces a good result will be accepted.

Discretion in the use of the pedals will be taken into account, but candidates who cannot reach the pedals easily will not be expected to use them.

Candidates whose hands are too small to play the music as written will not be penalised for "spreading" chords or omitting occasional notes at wide stretches provided the result is musically satisfactory.

Candidates at a centre may be required to play either on a horizontal or an upright pianoforte. Examiners will recognise the fact that the instrument may be one to which the candidates are unaccustomed.

Grade I (Primary)

1. (*a*) **Major Scales** from memory, with each hand separately, in the keys of C, G, D and F, two octaves. R.H. up and down: L.H. may, if the candidate prefers, be played down and up.

(*b*) **Broken Chords** from memory in the major keys of C, G and F, with each hand separately, starting from the lowest note (up and down) *and* from the highest note (down and up), according to both the following examples:—

(i)

and

(ii)

2. Three Pieces*:—

Either LIST A

1. **Healey Willan. Cuckoo Calls** (*Frederick Harris*)
2. **Handel. Minuet in F**

3(a). **Jessie Furze. Told in the Twilight** (*Ascherberg*)

or

(b). **Shostakovich. March. From Six Children's Pieces** (*Boosey & Hawkes*)

or LIST B

1. **Jeremiah Clarke. March. from At the Court of Queen Anne, ed. Fuller Maitland** (*Chester*)
2. **Purcell. Minuet, ed. Barclay Squire** (*Chester*)

3(a). **Stanford. Lullaby** (*Galliard*)

or

(b). **Philipp Jarnach. Duettino. From the New Piano Book, Vol. I** (*Schott*)

Selections may not be made from both lists, but as a further alternative to No. 3 in the chosen list, one of the following pieces may be played:—

Simone Plé. La Poupée Endormie. From Les Chants et Les Jeux (*United Music Publishers*)

Renie Stoym. Great Fun. From Special Purpose Pieces, Book 3 (*Freeman*)

3. Playing at Sight a melody of about eight bars in simple time in the major key of C, G or F in the treble and bass clefs for one hand at a time. It will be put before the candidate to read through and play.

As an aid to the reading he may, but need not, first clap or tap the time-values of the notes while counting aloud the number of beats in each bar or giving the French time-names at the speed at which he will play it; and/or count aloud while playing the actual notes.

4. Aural Tests for the Grade, see page 26.

* Published by the Board.

Grade II (Elementary)

1. Scales and Broken Chords, from memory:—

(*a*) **Major Scales** and **Minor Scales** (melodic *or* harmonic at candidate's choice): each hand separately, and hands together in similar motion one octave apart in the following keys:

C, G, D, A and F majors (two octaves);
A, E and D minors (one octave or two, at candidate's choice).

In **contrary** motion with both hands beginning and ending on the key-note (unison), in the key of C major only. One octave.

(*b*) **Chromatic Scale,** beginning on A♭, with each hand separately. One octave.

(*c*) **Broken Chords,** formed from the chords of C, G and F major, and A, E and D minor, with each hand separately, according to either of the patterns, at candidate's choice, in the following examples:—

(i) *or* (ii)

2. Three pieces*:—

Either **LIST A**

1. **Burgmüller. Study, Op. 100, No. 16**
2. **Hook. Country Dance, arr. Alec Rowley** (*Boosey & Hawkes*)

3(a). **Franck. Les Plaintes d'une Poupée** (*Schott*)
or
(b). **Henk Badings. Ballo gaio. From Reihe Kleiner Klavierstücke** (*Schott*)

or **LIST B**

1. **C. P. E. Bach. Allegro**
2. **Mozart. Minuet in F (K.5)**

3(a). **Jessie Furze. Robin on the Window-Sill. From From my Window** (*Freeman*)
or
(b). **Hindemith. Lied aus Wir bauen eine Stadt. From Von Bartók bis Stravinsky** (*Schott*)

Selections may not be made from both lists, but as a further alternative to No. 3 in the chosen list, one of the following pieces may be played:—

Harold Craxton. A Tuneful Study. From Two Studies for Piano (*Weinberger*)
Jessie Furze. Over the Dunes. From Windmill Land (*Weinberger*)

3. Playing at sight a few bars in the G and F clefs **with both hands together.**

4. Aural Tests for the Grade, see pages 26 and 27.

Grade III (Transitional)

1. Scales and Arpeggios from memory:—

(*a*) **Major Scales** and **Minor Scales** (melodic *or* harmonic at candidate's choice): two octaves, each hand separately and hands together in similar motion one octave apart in the following keys:

A, E, F, B♭, E♭, A♭ majors; A, E, D, G, C minors.

In **contrary** motion with both hands beginning and ending on the key-note (unison), in the major keys of E and E♭. One octave.

(*b*) **Chromatic Scales,** beginning on A♭, C and E, as named by the Examiner, with each hand separately. Two octaves.

(*c*) **Arpeggios**—the common chords of C, G and F major, and A, E and D minor, in root position only, with each hand separately. Two octaves.

2. Three Pieces*:—

Either LIST A

1. **Kabalevsky. Having Fun, ed. Alfred Mirovitch (*Boosey & Hawkes*)**
2. **Graupner. Air, arr. Martin Frey (*Hinrichsen*)**

3(a). **Dorothy Howell. Danse Levantine (*Chester*)**

or

(b). **Stravinsky. Larghetto. From Les Cinq Doigts (*Chester*)**

or LIST B

1. **Burgmüller. Study, Op. 100, No. 15**
2. **Gurlitt. Impromptu, Op. 224, No. 5**

3(a). **York Bowen. Minuet (*Weinberger*)**

or

(b). **Arnold Cooke. Pastorale (*Ricordi*)**

Selections may not be made from both lists, but as a further alternative to No. 3 in the chosen list, one of the following pieces may be played:—

Myers Foggin. Changing Guard (*Weinberger*)
Dunhill. No. 9 of Wheel of Progress, Book II (*Associated Board*)

3. Playing at sight.

4. Aural Tests for the Grade, see page 27.

---

* Published by the Board.

Grade IV (Lower)

1. Scales and Arpeggios, two octaves, from memory:—

(*a*) **Major Scales** and **Minor Scales** (melodic *or* harmonic at candidate's choice): each hand separately, and hands together in similar motion one octave apart in the following keys:

E, B, F♯, A♭, D♭ majors; E, B, F♯, C♯, C, F, B♭ minors

In **contrary** motion with both hands beginning and ending on the key-note (unison), in the major keys of E and E♭.

(*b*) **Chromatic Scales,** beginning on any note named by the Examiner, with each hand separately.

(*c*) **Arpeggios**—the common chords of C, G, D, A, E, F, B♭, E♭ and A♭ major and A, E and D minor, in root position only, with each hand separately.

2. Three Pieces*:—

Either LIST A

1. **W. F. Bach. Allegro Moderato, ed. Martin Frey** (*Bosworth*)
2. **Hasse. Signora Auretti's Dance, arr. Harold Craxton and Alfred Moffat** (*Cramer*)

3(a). **Sybil Barlow. Flight of the Bat** (*Weinberger*)

or

(b). **Darius Milhaud. Morning. From One Day** (*Schott*)

or LIST B

1. **William Boyce. Siciliana, arr. Harold Craxton and Alfred Moffat** (*Cramer*)
2. **Beethoven. Variations on a Swiss Air, omitting Var. 4**

3(a). **Schumann. Remembrance. From Album for the Young**

or

(b). **Bartók. Roumanian Folk Dance** (*Universal*)

Selections may not be made from both lists, but as a further alternative to No. 3 in the chosen list, one of the following pieces may be played:—

John B. McEwen. Andante. Second movement from Sonatina (*Oxford University Press*)
Philip G. Wilkinson. Dreams. From Playtime and Pageantry (*Augener*)

3. Playing at Sight.

4. Aural Tests for the Grade, see page 27.

Grade V (Higher)

1. Scales and Arpeggios, from memory:—

(*a*) **Major Scales** and **Minor Scales** (melodic *or* harmonic at candidate's choice) (three octaves): each hand separately, and hands together in similar motion one octave apart, **in all keys.**
In **contrary** motion (two octaves) with both hands beginning and ending on the key-note (unison), in the major keys of E, E♭ and A.

---

* Published by the Board.

(*b*) **Chromatic Scales** (three octaves); each hand separately, and hands together in similar motion one octave apart, beginning on any note named by the Examiner.
In **contrary** motion (two octaves) beginning and ending on C with the left hand and E with the right, a third apart.

(*c*) **Arpeggios** (two octaves)—all the major and minor common chords in root position only; each hand separately, and hands together in similar motion one octave apart.

2. Three Pieces*:—

Either LIST A

1. **Handel. Allemande from Suite No. 16**
2. **Haydn. Minuet and Trio from Sonata in D**
3(a). **Grieg. Little Bird. From Lyric Pieces, Book III**
or
(b). **Darius Milhaud. Mother. From A Child Loves (*Leeds Music*)**

or LIST B

1. **Telemann. Allemande from Klavierbüchlein for W. F. Bach**
2. **Mozart. Andante Espressivo, K.284a**
3(a). **William Alwyn. The Sea is angry. From Five by Ten (*Lengnick*)**
or
(b). **Ferenc Farkas. Correspondance. From Huit Pièces (*Mills Music*)**

Selections may not be made from both lists, but as a further alternative to No. 3 in the chosen list, one of the following pieces may be played:—

Festing. No. 1 of Two Jigs, arr. Harold Craxton and Alfred Moffat (*Cramer*)
Gordon Jacob. The Elephant's Child (*Associated Board*)

3. Playing at Sight.

4. Aural Tests for the Grade, see pages 27 and 28.

Grade VI (Intermediate)

1. Theory of Music, Grade V (Higher), must have been passed: see pages 12 and 21.

2. Scales and Arpeggios, from memory, in the keys specified in one of the following groups chosen by the candidate:—

Group I: C, E, A♭ majors; C, E, G♯ minors

Group II: D♭, F, A majors; C♯, F, A minors

Group III: D, F♯, B♭ majors and minors

Group IV: E♭, G, B majors and minors

(*a*) **Scales:—**

Major and minor, *both* melodic *and* harmonic (four octaves) with each hand separately;
with hands in similar motion one octave apart.

Major (two octaves).
in contrary motion, hands beginning and ending on the key-note (unison).

(*b*) **Chromatic Scales,** beginning on any note named by the Examiner:—

with each hand separately (four octaves);
with hands in similar motion one octave apart (four octaves);
in contrary motion, hands beginning and ending on the same note, unison (two octaves).

(*c*) **Arpeggios,** with each hand separately and with hands together an octave apart:—

(i) major and minor common chords (four octaves) in root position and in their inversions in the keys of the chosen group;

(ii) diminished seventh chords† (three octaves) beginning on any note named by the examiner without reference to kev

3. Four Pieces*:—

Either LIST A

1. **Loeillet. Gigue**
2. **Beethoven. Minuet and Trio from Sonata in E♭, Op. 31, No. 3**
3. **Schumann. May, charming May, Op. 68, No. 13**

4(a). **Bernard Stevens. Nocturne No. 2, from Five by Ten** (*Lengnick*)
or
(b). **Walter Schulthess. Praeludium, from The New Piano Book, Vol. II** (*Schott*)

or LIST B

1. **Avison. Concerto No. 12 in D; last movement**
2. **Mozart. First movement from Sonata in F, K.332**
3. **Edwin Benbow. Bagatelle** (*Cramer*)

4(a). **Delius. Mazurka** (*Universal*)
or
(b). **Shostakovich. No. 22 of 24 Preludes, Op. 34** (*Boosey & Hawkes*)

Selections may not be made from both lists, but as a further alternative to No. 4 in the chosen list, one of the following pieces may be played:—

Ivor R. Foster. A Summer Song (*Weinberger*)
Parry. Elizabeth. No. 2 of Shulbrede Tunes (*Augener*)

4. Playing at Sight.

5. Aural Tests for the Grade, see page 28.

---

† These are not confined to the keys in the group chosen for scales and common chord arpeggios.

Grade VII (Advanced)

1. Theory of Music, Grade V (Higher), must have been passed: see pages 12 and 21.

2. Scales and Arpeggios, from memory, in the keys specified in one of the following groups chosen by the candidate:—

GROUP I: A, C, E♭, F♯ majors and minors

GROUP II: B♭, D♭, E, G majors; B♭, C♯, E, G minors

GROUP III: B, D, F, A♭ majors; B, D, F, G♯ minors

(*a*) **Scales:**—

Major and minor, *both* melodic *and* harmonic (four octaves) with each hand separately;

with hands in similar motion one octave apart;

with hands in similar motion a third apart.

Major and harmonic minor (two octaves) in contrary motion, hands beginning and ending on the key-note (unison).

(*b*) **Chromatic Scales,** as in Grade VI.

(*c*) **Arpeggios,** with each hand separately and with hands together an octave apart:—

(i) major and minor common chords in root position and in their inversions (four octaves).

(ii) chords of the dominant seventh in root position only (three octaves).

3. Four Pieces*:—

Either LIST A

1. **Bach. Prelude in G, No. 15, Book I**
2. **Schumann. Grillen, Op. 12, No. 4**
3. **Chopin. Nocturne. Op. 72, No. 1**

4(a). **Scriabin. Prelude, Op. 13, No. 2** (*Boosey & Hawkes*)

or

(b). **Khachaturian. Dance** (*Boosey & Hawkes*)

or LIST B

1. **Scarlatti. Sonata in G minor, L.390**
2. **Haydn. First movement from Sonata in E♭**
3. **Schubert. Moment Musical, op. 94, No. 2**

4(a). **Lloyd Webber. Presto for Perseus** (*Ascherberg*)

or

(b). **Federico Mompou. Pour inspirer l'amour. From Charmes** (*Schott*)

(*continued*)

* Published by the Board.

Selections may not be made from both lists, but as a further alternative to No. 4 in the chosen list, one of the following pieces may be played:—

Frank Bridge. Valse Capricieuse (*Boosey & Hawkes*)

Philip Wilkinson. Mazurka (*Associated Board*)

4. Playing at Sight.

5. Aural Tests for the Grade, see pages 28 and 29.

Grade VIII (Final)

1. Theory of Music, Grade V (Higher), must have been passed: see pages 12 and 21.

2. Scales and Arpeggios, from memory, in the keys specified in one of the following groups chosen by the candidate:—

GROUP I: C, D, E, F♯, A♭, B♭ majors; C, D, E, F♯, G♯, B♭ minors

GROUP II: D♭, E♭, F, G, A, B majors; C♯, E♭, F, G, A, B minors

(*a*) **Scales,** legato or staccato as directed by the examiner:—

Major and minor, *both* melodic *and* harmonic (four octaves)
with each hand separately;
with hands in similar motion one octave apart;
with hands in similar motion a third or a sixth apart, at candidate's choice.

Major and harmonic minor (two octaves)
in contrary motion, hands beginning and ending on the key-note, either at their widest distance or at their closest point as required.

Major (two octaves)
with each hand separately in thirds (staccato only), beginning on the highest or lowest notes.

(*b*) **Chromatic Scales,** legato or staccato as directed, beginning on any note named by the Examiner:—

with each hand separately (four octaves);

in similar motion with hands one octave apart (four octaves);

in similar motion with hands a major or minor third apart (four octaves);

in contrary motion, hands beginning and ending on the same note, unison or an octave apart (two octaves).

(*c*) **Arpeggios,** legato only, in the same forms as set for Grade VII.

3. Three Pieces, one chosen by the candidate from each of the three groups A, B and C:—

GROUP A

1.*Bach. Prelude and Fugue in B♭ major, Book I, No. 21
2.*J. C. F. Bach. Fugue only from Fantasie and Fugue in F major
3. Handel. Gigue in G minor from Suite No. 9
4. Paul Hindemith. Interludium and Fuga No. 8 from Ludus Tonalis (*Schott*)

GROUP B (whole work)

1.*Beethoven. Sonata in F♯, Op. 78
2.*Beethoven. Andante in F
3.*Mendelssohn. Fantasia in F♯ minor, Op. 28
4.*Mozart. Sonata in B♭, K.333
5. Schumann. Novelette in F♯ minor, No. 8

GROUP C

1. Albeniz. Sevillanas (*Joseph Williams*)
2. Bartók. Ostinato. No. 146 in Mikrokosmos Vol. VI (*Boosey & Hawkes*)
3. Brahms. Intermezzo, Op. 117, No. 1 (*Lengnick*)
4. Frank Bridge. Capriccio No 1 (*Augener*)
5.*Chopin. Nocturne, Op. 32, No. 2
6. Debussy. Passepied, from Suite Bergamasque (*United Music Publishers*)
7. Ireland. Aubade (*Schott*)
8. Prokofiew. Prelude, Op. 12, No. 7 (*Hinrichsen*)
9. Ravel. Menuet from Le Tombeau de Couperin (*United Music Publishers*)
10. Bernard Stevens. No. 3 of Five Inventions (*Lengnick*)

4. Playing at Sight.

5. Aural Tests for the Grade, see page 29.

* Published by the Board.

PIANOFORTE DUETS

Two Performers at one Piano

There are three divisions, of which the Junior is appropriate for players approaching the standard of Grade V (Higher), Middle for players of Grade VI to VII, and Senior approaching Grade VIII.

The examination may last about 20 minutes in the Junior Division, and 25 minutes in the Middle and Senior Divisions.

Schedule of maximum marks:—

	Junior	Middle and Senior
Pieces 1	42	66
2	42	48
3	42	—
Playing at Sight	24	36
Total	150	150

Candidates may play in either position at their own choice, but must change places for one of the prepared pieces—whichever they choose.

The test of Playing at Sight will be in duet form, for both players together. They may briefly discuss it and indicate tempo to one another before beginning to play.

Both players will be under examination and marks will be awarded on the ensemble. 100 marks are required to pass, 120 to pass with Merit, and 130 to pass with Distinction, and a certificate will be issued to each player accordingly.

Junior Division

1. Playing at Sight.

2. Three Pieces. Candidates must prepare one of the following three lists:—

Either LIST A*

Mozart. Second Movement from Sonata in D (K.381)
Grieg. Norwegian Dance, Op. 35, No. 2
Bizet. Petit Mari, Petite Femme. No. 11 from Jeux d'Enfants

or LIST B

Weber. March. Op. 3, No. 5 (*Associated Board*)
Mozart. First Movement from Sonatina in B♭ (K.240) (*Peters 4456*)
Inghelbrecht. A mon beau chateau. From La Nursery, Book IV (*United Music Publishers*)

---

* The duets in List A are published together in one book by the Board. Those in Lists B and C can only be obtained separately.

or LIST C

Schubert. Kinder-Marsch (*Augener*)
Schumann. Garden Melody, Op. 85, No. 3 (*Augener*)
William Walton. Trumpet Tune. No. 10, Book II, from Duets for Children (*Oxford University Press*)

Middle Division

1. **Playing at Sight.**

2. **Two Pieces.** Candidates must prepare one of the following lists:—

Either LIST A*

Beethoven. Sonata in D, Op. 6
Bizet. Trompette et Tambour. No. 6 from Jeux d'Enfants

or LIST B

J. C. Bach. Sonata in F, Op. 18, No. 6 (*Associated Board*)
Debussy. En Bateau, from Petite Suite (*United Music Publishers*)

or LIST C

Mozart. Sonata in C (K.19D) (*Oxford University Press*)
Fauré. Kitty-Valse, Op. 56, No. 4 (*United Music Publishers*)

Senior Division

1. **Playing at Sight.**

2. **Two Pieces.** Candidates must prepare one of the following lists:—

Either LIST A*

Schubert. Fantasie in F minor, Op. 103
Dvořák. Slavonic Dance in A♭, Op. 46, No. 6

or LIST B

Schubert. Grand Sonata, Op. 30 (*Associated Board*)
Debussy. Ballet, from Petite Suite (*United Music Publishers*)

or LIST C

Mozart. Sonata in B♭ (K.358) (*Augener*)
Francis Poulenc. Sonata (*Chester*)

ORGAN

Grades IV (Lower) to VIII (Final) only

Candidates will, if possible, be examined on an organ to which they are accustomed, provided it is easily accessible from one of the regular examination centres and that the candidate (or his teacher) will arrange for it to be available at a time to fit in with the examiner's other commitments. It should have an orthodox console with at least two manuals. drawstops or tablets, radiating pedal-board, swell pedal and the usual couplers; if there is any doubt of the suitability of the organ, its specification should be reported to the Board prior to entry.

The Board does not publish specimen sight-reading tests for Organ. The sight-reading tests vary in standard from a melodious four-part hymn with pedals (Grade IV) to pieces comparable in difficulty to Bach's eight short fugues or the easier chorale preludes (Grade VIII). The transposition tests in Grades VII and VIII are of the nature of simple four-part hymns.

Schedule of maximum marks:—

	Grade IV, V & VI	VII & VIII
Scales	18	—
Studies and Pieces—1	30	30
2	30	30
3	30	30
Playing at Sight	24	24
Transposition	—	18
Aural Tests	18	18
Total ..	150	150

Grade IV (Lower)

1. Scales, from memory, in the major and minor (both melodic and harmonic) keys of G, D and B♭:—

(*a*) with both hands (without pedals), two octaves;
(*b*) with the feet alone, one octave;
(*c*) with left hand and feet in contrary motion, one octave, major scales only.

2. Three Pieces†. Candidates must prepare the whole of one of the following lists, either A or B or C; they may not select from separate lists.

Either LIST A

Bach. Chorale Prelude "Vom Himmel hoch", BWV. 606 (*Novello XV, p. 21; Peters V, p. 53*)

Mendelssohn. Second movement (*Andante Religioso*) from Sonata No. 4 (*Novello or Peters*)

Henry Coleman. Prelude from An Easy Album (*Oxford University Press*)

or LIST B

Bach. First movement of Pastorale in F, BWV. 590 (*Novello XII, p. 102; Peters I, p. 88*)

Buxtehude. Chorale Prelude "Puer natus in Bethlehem" from The Progressive Organist, Book I, ed. C. H. Trevor (*Elkin*)

Stanley. Adagio in E minor (No. 2 of Three Pieces), ed. Henry Coates (*Joseph Williams*)

or LIST C

Bach. Prelude in E minor. No. 3 of Eight Short Preludes and Fugues, BWV. 555 (*Novello I, p. 8; Peters VIII, p. 54*)

Merkel. Fughetta, Op. 37, No. 2, from The Progressive Organist, Book I, ed. C. H. Trevor (*Elkin*)

Healey Willan. Intermezzo, from Miniature Suite (*Ascherberg*)

3. Playing at Sight.

4. Aural Tests for the Grade, see page 27.

Grade V (Higher)

1. Scales, from memory, in the major and minor (both melodic and harmonic) keys of C, E♭ and D♭:—

(*a*) with both hands (without pedals), two octaves;

(*b*) with the feet alone, two octaves;

(*c*) with left hand and feet in contrary motion, one octave, major scales only.

2. Three Pieces†. Candidates must prepare the whole of one of the following lists, either A or B or C; they may not select from separate lists.

Either LIST A

Telemann. Fugue No. 5, from The Progressive Organist, Book I, ed. C. H. Trevor (*Elkin*)

Karg-Elert. "O my soul, rejoice", No 1 of Fourteen Chorale-Improvisations, Op. 65 (*British & Continental Music Agencies*)

Armstrong Gibbs. Jubilate Deo. No. 3, Book I of Six Sketches (*Oxford University Press*)

or LIST B

Mendelssohn. Fugue from Sonata No. 6 in D minor (*Novello or Peters*)

William Harris. Prelude, No. 1 of Four Short Pieces (*Novello*)

S. Wesley. Gavotte, No. 3 of Three Short Pieces (*Novello*)

or LIST C

Bach. Fugue only in G minor. No. 6 of Eight Short Preludes and Fugues, BWV. 558 (*Novello I, p. 18; Peters VIII, p. 64*)

Gordon Slater. Prelude "St. Botolph" (*Oxford University Press*)

Eric Thiman. Finale in D minor, from An Easy Album (*Oxford University Press*)

3. Playing at Sight.

4. Aural Tests for the Grade, see pages 27 and 28.

Grade VI (Intermediate)

1. Theory of Music, Grade V (Higher), must have been passed: see pages 12 and 21.

2. Scales, etc.

(*a*) with both hands, from memory, in the major and minor (both melodic and harmonic) keys of E, F and F♯, two octaves (without pedals);

(*b*) Pedal Solo from Prelude in C major by Bach (*Novello VII, p. 74; Peters IV, p. 2; also available separately, price 9d., on application to the Board*).

---

† The music required for the Organ examinations is **NOT published by the Board** but may be obtained through a music seller.

3. Three Pieces†. Candidates must prepare the whole of one of the following lists, either A or B or C; they may not select from separate lists.

Either LIST A

Bach. Chorale Prelude "Vater Unser im Himmelreich", BWV. 737 (*Novello XIX, p. 12; Peters VII, p. 66*)

Vaughan Williams. Romanza, from Two Preludes on Welsh Folk Songs (*Oxford University Press*)

Mendelssohn. Fugue in C major, from Sonata No. 2 in C minor (*Novello or Peters*)

or LIST B

Bach. Fugue in G major, BWV. 576 (*Novello XII, p. 86; Peters IX, p. 12*)

Darke. Andantino, from A Little Organ Book (*Ascherberg*)

Karg-Elert. "I thank Thee, dearest Lord." No. 9 of Fourteen Chorale-Improvisations, Op. 65 (*British & Continental Music Agencies*)

or LIST C

Bach. Prelude and Fugue in E minor, BWV. 533 (*Novello II, p. 44; Peters III, p. 88*)

Mendelssohn. Second movement (*Andante con moto*) **from Sonata No. 5 in D major** (*Novello or Peters*)

Stanley. Allegro only, from Introduction and Allegro, arr. Coleman (*Cramer*)

4. Playing at Sight.

5. Aural Tests for the Grade, see page 28.

Grade VII (Advanced)

1. Theory of Music, Grade V (Higher), must have been passed: see pages 12 and 21.

2. Three Pieces†. Candidates must prepare the whole of one of the following lists, either A or B or C; they may not select from separate lists.

Either LIST A

Bach. Fugue only, from Prelude and Fugue in A, BWV. 536 (*Novello III, p. 66; Peters II, p. 16*)

Healey Willan. Chorale Prelude on a Melody by Orlando Gibbons. No. 3 of Six Chorale Preludes (*Oxford University Press*)

Rheinberger. First Movement of Sonata in G (Pastoral), Op. 88 (*Novello*)

or LIST B

Rheinberger. Fughetta No. 1, Op. 123a, ed. Lloyd Webber (*Hinrichsen 47*)

Harwood. Communion in F major on Hymn Tune "Irish" (*Novello*)

Handel. First movement of Concerto in G minor, No. 5, arr. H. G. Ley (*Stainer & Bell*)

(*continued*)

---

† The music required for the Organ examinations is NOT published by the Board, but may be obtained through a music seller.

***or* LIST C**

Bach. Prelude in F minor, BWV. 534 (*Novello VI, p. 21; Peters II, p. 29*)
Franck. Prelude only, from Prelude, Fugue and Variation (*Novello*)
Stanford. On a Theme of Orlando Gibbons (Song 24). No. 4 of Six Short Preludes and Postludes, Op. 105. Second Set (*Stainer & Bell*)

3. **Playing** a piece **at sight,** and **transposing** a simple hymn tune (manuals only) a tone or semitone higher or lower.

4. **Aural Tests** for the Grade, see pages 28 and 29.

Grade VIII (Final)

1. **Theory of Music,** Grade V (Higher), must have been passed: see pages 12 and 21.

2. **Three Pieces**†, one chosen by the candidate from each of the three groups A, B and C:—

GROUP A

1. **Bach. Fugue in G minor, BWV. 578 (*Novello III, p. 84; Peters IV, p. 46*)**
2. **Bach. Fugue only from Prelude and Fugue in C, BWV. 545 (*Novello III, p. 72; Peters II, p. 4*)**
3. **Bach. First movement from Sonata No. 1 in E♭, BWV. 525 (*Novello IV, p. 88; Peters I, p. 2*)**

GROUP B

1. **Herbert Howells. Psalm-Prelude, No. 2, Op. 32 (*Novello*)**
2. **Parry. Chorale Prelude "Martyrdom", from Seven Chorale Preludes, Second Set (*Novello*)**
3. **Percy Whitlock. Fidelis, No. 3 of Four Extemporisations (*Oxford University Press*)**

GROUP C

1. **Gordon Slater. An Easter Alleluya (*Oxford University Press*)**
2. **Gabriel Pierné. Prelude, from Three Pieces (*United Music Publishers*)**
3. **Stanford. No. 6 of Six Short Preludes and Postludes, Second Set, Op. 105 (*Stainer & Bell*)**

3. **Playing** a piece **at sight,** and **transposing** a hymn tune (manuals only) a tone or semitone higher or lower.

4. **Aural Tests** for the Grade, see page 29.

STRINGED INSTRUMENTS

Candidates must provide their own accompanists, who may remain in the room only whilst actually engaged in accompanying. A teacher may act as an accompanist but the Examiner will not. The tests of Playing at Sight will be given without accompaniment.

In Grades I to V the teacher or accompanist may tune the candidate's instrument before the examination begins. The Examiner should not be expected to do so. In Grades VI to VIII candidates will be required to tune their own instruments. Candidates should provide themselves with music stands if they require them.

Candidates are not compelled to adhere to the fingering indicated; any good practical fingering will be accepted. In Grades I and II candidates will not be expected to play in any but the first position except in scales or arpeggios where necessary. By Grade V candidates should have acquired some skill in vibrato.

Intonation, production and quality of tone, bowing and finger action, and posture will be taken into account in the marking of the Pieces and Studies, and of Scales, Arpeggios and Exercises.

Schedule of maximum marks:—

Grade	I-V	VI, VII	VIII
Pieces and Studies:—1	27	27	30
2	27	27	30
3	27	15	27
4	—	15	—
Exercises	15	—	—
Scales }	18	15	27
Arpeggios }		15	
Sight Reading	18	18	18
Aural Tests	18	18	18
Total	150	150	150

VIOLIN

Grade I (Primary)

1. Three Works*:—

Either LIST A

Joan Lovell and Gertrude Reeks. Burlesque, from Tuning Up (*Oxford University Press*)

Carse. Waltz Time, from The Fiddler's Nursery (*Augener*)

Herbert Kinsey. Study in A from Preliminary Studies

or LIST B

Carse. Minuet, from The Fiddler's Nursery (*Augener*)

Szelényi. Playsong, from Twenty-four Easy Little Concert Pieces for Violin (*Boosey and Hawkes*)

Woof. Study in G from Fifty Elementary Studies

Selections may not be made from both lists, but as an alternative to the *second* piece in either list, one of the following may be chosen:—

Carse. Romance. No. 7 of First String Tunes (*Augener*)

Eleanor Murray. Down by the River. No. 4 of Still More Tunes for my Violin (*Boosey and Hawkes*)

Extract from the Beethoven Septet, from Anderson's Fourth Violin Album (*Bosworth*)

2. The **Exercises** in the book of Pieces* for this grade.

3. Scales and **Arpeggios***, from memory:—

(*a*) **Major Scales** in the key of G (two octaves) and in the keys of G, D and A (one octave, starting on open strings); separate bows, as example below:—

Also the same Scales, but with the quavers slurred two to a bow.

(*b*) **Arpeggios**—the major common chords of G, D and A (one octave, starting on open strings); separate bows only, as example below:—

4. Playing at sight a melody in simple time in the major key of C, G or D. It will be put before the candidate to read through and play.

As an aid to the reading he may, but need not, first clap or tap the time-values of the notes while counting aloud the number of beats in each bar or giving the French time-names at the speed at which he will play it; and/or count aloud while playing the actual notes.

5. Aural Tests for the Grade, see page 26.

Grade II (Elementary)

1. Three Works*:—

Either LIST A

Handel, arr. James Brown. Dance for a Masque. No. 7 of Easy for Both (*Stainer and Bell*)
Irish Air, Kitty of Coleraine, from Anderson's Fourth Violin Album (*Bosworth*)
Herbert Kinsey. Study in D minor, from Elementary Progressive Studies, First Set

or LIST B

Scottish Air, Come o'er the Stream, from Anderson's Fourth Violin Album (*Bosworth*)
Old French, arr. James Brown. Chansonette. No. 18 of Easy for Both (*Stainer and Bell*)
Woof. Study in B♭ from Fifty Elementary Studies

Selections may not be made from both lists, but as an alternative to the *second* piece in either list, one of the following may be chosen:—

Carse. Dance Steps, from The Fiddler's Nursery (*Augener*)
Purcell. Ayre *or* **Schumann. A Little Piece** } **from First Book of Graded Classical and Romantic Pieces, arr. Watson Forbes** (*Oxford University Press*)

2. The **Exercises** in the book of Pieces* for this Grade.

---

* Published by the Board.

3. Scales and Arpeggios*, from memory:—

(*a*) **Major Scales** in the keys of G, A and B♭ (two octaves), and minor scales (harmonic *or* melodic at candidate's choice) in the keys of G, D and A (one octave, starting on open strings):—

(i) Separate bows, as example in Grade I;

(ii) with the quavers slurred two to a bow.

(*b*) **Arpeggios**—the common chords of G and A major (two octaves) and of G, D and A minor (one octave, starting on open strings); separate bows, as example in Grade I.

4. Playing at Sight.

5. Aural Tests for the Grade, see pages 26 and 27.

Grade III (Transitional)

1. Three Works*†:—

Either LIST A

David Stone. March in D, from Eight Pieces in the third position (*Novello*)
Gluck. Andante, from Die alte Geige (*Universal*)
Hullah Brown. Seed Time, from Twenty-one Melodic Violin Studies (*Joseph Williams*)

or LIST B

Weber, arr. Moffat. Waltz, from Old Fiddle Pieces (*Schott*)
Corelli, arr. Moffat. Largo affettuoso, from Old Fiddle Pieces (*Schott*)
Neil Mackay. Gavotte, from A Tuneful Introduction to the Third Position (*Augener*)

Selections may not be made from both lists, but as an alternative to the *second* piece in either list, one of the following may be chosen:—

Humperdinck, arr. Robjohns. Sleep Song from Hansel and Gretel (*Schott*)
Handel. Slow Music for a Ballet. No. 4 of Easy for Both (*Stainer and Bell*)
Chopin. Choral, from Op. 37, No. 1. (*First Book of Graded Classical and Romantic Pieces, arr. Watson Forbes. Oxford University Press*)

2. The **Exercises** in the book of Pieces* for this Grade.

3. Scales and Arpeggios*, from memory (two octaves) in the following keys:—

G, A, B♭, D majors; G, A, B minors

(*a*) **Scales,** major and minor (harmonic *or* melodic at candidate's choice):—

(i) Separate bows, as example in Grade I;

(ii) with the quavers slurred two to a bow.

(*b*) **Arpeggios**—the major and minor common chords; separate bows, as example in Grade I (two octaves).

4. Playing at Sight.

5. **Aural Tests** for the Grade, see page 27.

Grade IV (Lower)

1. Three Works*†:—

Either LIST A

Bach. Polacca, arr. Watson Forbes
David Stone. Festive Dance, from Eight Pieces in the third position (*Novello*)
Sevcik. Study No. 13 in F, Op. 2, Part 2 (*Bosworth*)

or LIST B

Corelli. Prelude from Sonata No. 9 in A, arr. Watson Forbes. (*Oxford University Press*)
Irish Air, The Rakes of Mallow (60 *Graded Pieces, Second Series. Augener*)
Carse. Study in G from Progressive Studies, Book III (*Augener*)

Selections may not be made from both lists, but as an alternative to the *second* piece in either list, one of the following may be chosen:—

David Stone. Country Dance. No. 4 from Eight Pieces in the third position (*Novello*)
Szelényi. In the Circus *or* The Hen and the Cock. From Twenty-four Easy Little Concert Pieces for Violin, Book II (*Boosey and Hawkes*)
Dunhill. Gavotte Plaintive. No. 1 of Five Lyrical Pieces (*Joseph Williams*)

2. The **Exercises** in the book of Pieces* for this Grade.

3. Scales and Arpeggios*, from memory (two octaves) in the following keys:—

A♭, B♭, C, D majors; B, C, D minors

(*a*) **Scales,** major and minor (harmonic *or* melodic at candidate's choice):—
(i) Separate bows, as example in Grade I;
(ii) Slurred, two beats to a bow, as in the following example:—

(*b*) **Arpeggios**—the major and minor common chords (two octaves);
(i) Separate bows, as example in Grade I;
(ii) Slurred three notes to a bow, as in following example:—

4. Playing at Sight.

5. Aural Tests for the Grade, see page 27.

* Published by the Board.
† See page 88 for gramophone recording.

Grade V (Higher)

1. Three Works*:—

Either LIST A

Haydn. Tema con Variazioni, from Die alte Geige (*Universal*)
Christopher le Fleming. Air only, from Air and Dance. (Without 8va and double stopping) (*Chester*)
Sevcik. 40 Variations, Op. 3. The Theme and Variations 1, 6 and 7 (*Bosworth*)

or LIST B

Schubert. Waltz, arr. Peggy Radmall (*Chester*)
Somervell. The Dove (60 *Graded Teaching Pieces, Second Series. Augener*)
Herbert Kinsey. Study in A from Elementary Progressive Studies, Third Set

Selections may not be made from both lists, but as an alternative to the *second* piece in either list, one of the following may be chosen:—

Tartini. Andante Cantabile, arr. Niso Ticciati (*Oxford University Press*)
Palmgren. Berceuse, arr. Peggy Radmall (*Chester*)
Delius. Serenade from Hassan (*Boosey and Hawkes*)

2. The **Exercises** in the book of Pieces* for this Grade.

3. **Scales and Arpeggios***, from memory, in the following keys:—

B, C, D, E♭, E majors; B, C, D, E minors

(*a*) **Scales,** major and minor (harmonic *or* melodic at candidate's choice) (two octaves):—

(i) Separate bows, as example in Grade I;
(ii) Slurred, two beats to a bow, as in example in Grade IV.

(*b*) **Arpeggios**—the major and minor common chords (two octaves);

(i) Separate bows, as example in Grade I;
(ii) Slurred three notes to a bow, as example in Grade IV.

(*c*) **Chromatic Scales** starting on open strings G, D and A (one octave); separate bows.

4. **Playing at Sight.**

5. **Aural Tests** for the Grade, see pages 27 and 28.

Grade VI (Intermediate)

1. **Theory of Music,** Grade V (Higher), must have been passed: see pages 12 and 21.

2. Four Works*:—

Either LIST A

Corelli. Adagio Cantabile and Giga from Sonata No. 5 in G minor, Op. 5 (*Augener*)
Jenkinson. Elfentanz (*Bosworth*)
Woof. Study in B♭ from Thirty Studies of Moderate Difficulty
Herbert Kinsey. Study in B minor from Elementary Progressive Studies, Third Set

or LIST B

Handel. Second movement, *Allegro,* **from Sonata in F**
Weber, arr. Burmester. Waltz No. 1 (*Hinrichsen*)
Woof. Study in E minor from Thirty Studies of Moderate Difficulty
Mazas. Study in A minor, Op. 36, No. 2

Selections may not be made from both lists, but as an alternative to the *second* piece in either list, one of the following may be chosen:—

Mozart. Gavotte in F (*Schott*)
Kreisler. Liebesleid (*Schott*)
Albeniz. Tango, arr. Watson Forbes (*Oxford University Press*)

3. Scales and Arpeggios*, from memory: (*a*) and (*b*) in the keys specified in one of the following groups chosen by the candidate:—

GROUP I: G, B♭, C, E♭, F♯ majors; G, B, C, E♭, F♯ minors
GROUP II: G, B♭, D♭, E, F majors; G, B, C♯, E, F minors

(*a*) **Scales,** major and minor (*both* melodic *and* harmonic). Major scales in the keys of G and B♭ and minor scales in the keys of G and B, three octaves; the other scales two octaves only.

(i) Separate bows, even notes, as following examples:—

Two octaves

Three octaves

(ii) Slurred bowing, seven notes to a bow, as following example:—

(*b*) **Arpeggios**—the major and minor common chords. Arpeggios of G major and minor, three octaves; the other arpeggios two octaves only.

(i) Separate bows, as example in Grade I;
(ii) Slurred, three notes to a bow, as example in Grade IV.

(*c*) **Dominant Seventh** in the key of C (starting on the note G), two octaves; separate bows, even notes, as following example:—

(*d*) **Chromatic Scales** beginning on G, A and B♭, two octaves; slurred bowing, four or six notes to a bow at candidate's choice.

4. Playing at Sight.

5. Aural Tests for the Grade, see page 28.

* Published by the Board.

Grade VII (Advanced)

1. Theory of Music, Grade V (Higher), must have been passed: see pages 12 and 21.

2. Four Works*:—

Either LIST A

Mozart. Theme and Variations from Sonata No. 9 in F, K.377
Dvořák. Bagatelle, Op. 47, No. 3, arr. Watson Forbes (*Hinrichsen*)
Fiorillo. No. 7 from Thirty-six Studies
Viardot. No. 16 in D from L'Archet, 20 Studies for Violin (*United Music Publishers*)

or LIST B

Veracini. Second movement, *Allegro moderato,* **from Sonata in E minor, Op. 2, No. 8**
Dvořák. Larghetto from Sonatina Op. 100, arr. Watson Forbes
Mazas. Study in B♭, Op. 36, Book II, No. 38
Viardot. No. 13 in D minor from L'Archet, 20 Studies for Violin (*United Music Publishers*)

Selections may not be made from both lists, but as an alternative to the *second* piece in either list, one of the following may be chosen:—

Wieniawski. Dudziarz Mazurka, Op. 19, No. 2 (*Schott*)
Porpora-Kreisler. Minuet (*Schott*)
François Schubert. Le Papillon. No. 7 of Twelve Bagatelles, Op. 13 (*Schott*)

3. Scales and Arpeggios*, from memory; (*a*) and (*b*) in the keys specified in one of the following groups chosen by the candidate:—

GROUP I: G, A, B, D♭ majors; G, A, B, C♯ minors

GROUP II: A♭, B♭, C, D majors; G♯, B♭, C, D minors

(*a*) **Scales,** major and minor (*both* melodic *and* harmonic), three octaves.

(i) Separate bows, even notes, at a fairly quick pace, as example in Grade VI;

(ii) Slurred, seven notes to a bow, as example in Grade VI.

(*b*) **Arpeggios**—the major and minor common chords, three octaves.

(i) Separate bows, even notes, as example in Grade I;

(ii) Slurred, one bow ascending and one bow descending, as in following example:—

(*c*) **Dominant Sevenths,** Group I *or* Group II; i.e., the same group as already chosen for the scales and arpeggios (two octaves):—

GROUP I: starting on G, A, B, D♭ (keys of C, D, E, G♭)

GROUP II: starting on A♭, B♭, C, D (keys of D♭, E♭, F, G)

(i) Separate bows, even notes, as example in Grade VI;

(ii) Slurred, even notes, four notes to a bow.

---

* Published by the Board.

(*d*) **Chromatic Scales** starting on the notes specified in the chosen group of the scales and arpeggios, two octaves; slurred bowing, twelve notes to a bow.

4. Playing at Sight.

5. Aural Tests for the Grade, see pages 28 and 29.

Grade VIII (Final)

1. Theory of Music, Grade V (Higher), must have been passed: see pages 12 and 21.

2. Three Works†, one chosen by the candidate from each of the three groups A, B and C:—

GROUP A

1. **Bach. First and fourth movements, *Allegro* and *Gigue*, from Sonata in E minor (*Peters*)**
2. **Smetana. Aus der Heimat No. 2 (*Peters 2634*)**
3. **William Walton. Scherzetto. No. 2 of Two Pieces (*Oxford University Press*)**
4. **Mozart. Third movement, *Rondo*, without cadenza, from Concerto in G (K.216) (*Peters 2193L*)**

GROUP B

1. **Brahms. Second movement, *Adagio*, from Sonata in D minor, Op. 108 (*Schott*)**
2. **Schubert. Sonatina No. 3 in G minor, Op. 137 (whole work) (*Peters*)**
3. **Edmund Rubbra. Second movement, *Lament*, from Sonata No. 2 (*Oxford University Press*)**
4. **Jean Françaix. Sonatine (1934). First movement, *Vivace*, without 8va ad lib. (*Schott*)**

GROUP C

1. **Fiorillo. No. 15 of 36 Etudes (top bowing) (*Augener*)**
2. **Viardot. No. 8 in G from L'Archet, 20 Studies for Violin (*United Music Publishers*)**
3. **Mazas. No. 49 in E♭ of Brilliant Studies, Op. 36, Book II (*Augener*)**
4. **Rode. No. 18 in F minor of 24 Caprices (*Peters*)**

3. Scales and Arpeggios*, from memory, in all the keys set in Grade VII (*both* groups), i.e. from G to D inclusive:—

(*a*) Scales, major and minor
(*b*) Arpeggios
(*d*) **Chromatic Scales**
} Compass and bowing as in Grade VII

(*c*) **Dominant Sevenths,** two octaves, in the keys set in Grade VII, *both* groups: (i) separate bows, even notes; (ii) slurred, even notes, eight notes to a bow.

(*e*) **Scales in Double Notes,** one octave; B♭ major in thirds and in sixths, D major in octaves; separate bows.

4. Playing at Sight.

5. Aural Tests for the Grade, see page 29.

---

† The music required for Grade VIII (Final) Violin Examination is NOT published by the Board, but may be obtained through a music seller.

VIOLA

Grades II to VIII only

See page 46 for marks, and for rules concerning accompaniment, tuning, fingering and playing at sight.

A candidate may play on a Violin strung as a Viola.

Grade II (Elementary)

1. Three Works†:—

Either LIST A

Joan Lovell. Scherzino, No. 35, *and* **Bagatelle, No. 26, from Forty-four Easy Tunes for Viola and Piano** (*Oxford University Press*)

Herbert Kinsey. No. 2 in C from Easy Progressive Studies for Viola, Set II (*Associated Board*)

or LIST B

Eleanor Murray and Phillis Tate. Study in C, No. 6, *and* **March, No. 8, from The New Viola Albums, Book I** (*Oxford University Press*)

Campagnoli. No. 9 in B♭ (top line only) from Kreuz Select Studies for The Viola, Book I (*Augener 7657a*)

Selections may not be made from both lists, but as an alternative to the *second* piece in either list, the following may be chosen:—

Schumann. A Distant Land, Op. 15, No. 1, from Scenes of Childhood. (*No. 2 from A First Year Classical Album for Viola Players by Watson Forbes. Oxford University Press*)

2. Exercises: Set I of the 1963 edition for this Grade (*Associated Board*).

3. Scales and Arpeggios, from memory:—

(*a*) **Major Scales** in the keys of C and D (two octaves), and **Minor Scales** (harmonic *or* melodic at candidate's choice) in the keys of C and D (one octave, starting on open strings); separate bows, as example in Violin Grade I.
Also the same scales, but with the quavers slurred two to a bow.

(*b*) **Arpeggios**—the common chords of C and D major (two octaves) and of C and D minor (one octave, starting on open strings); separate bows only, as example in Violin Grade I.

4. Playing at sight.

5. Aural Tests for the Grade, see pages 26 and 27.

Grade III (Transitional)

1. Three Works†:—

Either LIST A

C. P. E. Bach. Allegretto in G, No. 3, *and* **Poco Andante in D, No. 1, from Three Little Pieces, arr. Peggy Radmall** (*Chester*)

Carse. Study No. 1 in C from Viola School, Book II (*Augener 7655B*)

---

† The music required for the Viola Examinations, except where stated, is NOT published by the Board, but may be obtained through a music seller.

or LIST B

Eleanor Murray and Phillis Tate. Hornpipe, No. 1, *and* Sarabande, No. 6, from The New Viola Albums, Book II (*Oxford University Press*)
Herbert Kinsey. No. 3 in B♭ of Easy Progressive Studies for Viola, Set II (*Associated Board*)

Selections may not be made from both lists, but as an alternative to the *second* piece in either list, the following may be chosen:—

Haydn. Romance from Symphony 85 (*No. 10 of A First Year Classical Album for Viola Players by Watson Forbes. Oxford University Press*)

2. Exercises: Set I of the 1963 edition for this Grade (*Associated Board*).

3. Scales and Arpeggios, from memory (two octaves) in the following keys:—

C, D, E♭, G majors; C, D, E minors

(*a*) **Scales,** major and minor (harmonic *or* melodic at candidate's choice).
(i) Separate bows, as example Violin Grade I;
(ii) with the quavers slurred two to a bow.

(*b*) **Arpeggios**—the major and minor common chords; separate bows, as example in Violin Grade I (two octaves).

4. Playing at Sight.

5. Aural Tests for the Grade, see page 27.

Grade IV (Lower)

1. Three Works†:—(Position work in the pieces desirable).

Either LIST A

Handel. Tempo di Gavotta, Op. 1, No. 2 *and* **Mozart. Larghetto from Divertimento K.229** — *Nos. 8 and 5 from A Second Year Classical Album for Viola Players by Watson Forbes* (*Oxford University Press*)
Herbert Kinsey. No. 13 in D of Easy Progressive Studies for Viola, Set II (*Associated Board*)

or LIST B

John Dyer. On the Serpentine (*Associated Board*)
Philip Browne. David of the White Rock (*Joseph Williams*)
Carse. Study No. 9 in D from Viola School, Book II (*Augener 7655B*)

Selections may not be made from both lists, but as an alternative to the *second* piece in either list, the following may be chosen:—

Beethoven. Liebeslied. No. 9 of Old Masters for Young Players, arr. Moffat and Palaschko (*Schott*)

2. Exercises: Set I of the 1963 edition for this Grade (*Associated Board*).

3. Scales and Arpeggios, from memory (two octaves) in the following keys:—

D♭, E♭, F, G majors; E, F, G minors

(*a*) **Scales,** major and minor (harmonic *or* melodic at candidate's choice).

(i) Separate bows, as example in Violin Grade I;

(ii) Slurred, two beats to a bow, as example in Violin Grade IV.

(*b*) **Arpeggios**—the major and minor common chords (two octaves).

(i) Separate bows, as example in Violin Grade I;

(ii) Slurred, three notes to a bow, as example in Violin Grade IV.

4. Playing at Sight.

5. Aural Tests for the Grade, see page 27.

Grade V (Higher)

1. Three Works†:—

Either LIST A

Tchaikovsky. Chanson Triste, arr. Watson Forbes (*Chester*)
Howard Ferguson. Nos. 1 and 2 of Four Short Pieces (*Boosey and Hawkes*)
Herbert Kinsey. No. 15 in G of Easy Progressive Studies for Viola, Set II (*Associated Board*)

or LIST B

Weber. Serenata (*Schott 10653*)
Ravel. Pavane pour une infante défunte (*Schott*)
Wessely. Study No. 48 in E♭ from Practical Viola School, Book I (*Joseph Williams*)

Selections may not be made from both lists, but as an alternative to the *second* piece in either list, the following may be chosen:—

Eleanor Murray and Phillis Tate. Rondino. No. 4 from The New Viola Albums, Book III (*Oxford University Press*)

2. Exercises: Set I of the 1963 edition for this Grade (*Associated Board*).

3. Scales and Arpeggios, from memory, in the following keys:—

E, F, G, A majors and minors

(*a*) **Scales,** major and minor (harmonic *or* melodic at candidate's choice), two octaves.

(i) Separate bows, as example in Violin Grade I;

(ii) Slurred, two beats to a bow, as example in Violin Grade IV.

(*b*) **Arpeggios**—the major and minor common chords (two octaves).

(i) Separate bows, as example in Violin Grade I;

(ii) Slurred, three notes to a bow, as example in Violin Grade IV.

(*c*) **Chromatic Scales** starting on open strings C, G and D (one octave); separate bows.

4. Playing at Sight.

5. Aural Tests for the Grade, see pages 27 and 28.

---

† The music required for the Viola Examinations, except where stated, is NOT published by the Board but may be obtained through a music seller.

Grade VI (Intermediate)

1. Theory of Music, Grade V (Higher), must have been passed: see pages 12 and 21.

2. Four Works†:—

Either LIST A

Schumann. No. 1 in D minor from Märchenbilder, Op. 113 (*Peters*)
Viotti. Allegretto piu tosto. No. 2 of Two Serenade Movements, arr Peggy Radmall (*Chester*)
Carse. No. 11 in D minor and No. 18 in D from Viola School, Book IV(*Augener 7655D*)

or LIST B

Mendelssohn. Song without Words, Op. 19, No. 1, arr. Watson Forbes (*Chester*)
Mozart. Gavotte, arr. Franz Reis (*Schott*)
Campagnoli. Nos. 6 and 17 from Kreuz Select Studies Book II (*Augener 7657B*)

Selections may not be made from both lists, but as an alternative to the *second* piece in either list, the following may be chosen:—

John Dyer. In the Row (*Associated Board*)

3. Scales and Arpeggios, from memory, (*a*) and (*b*) in the keys specified in one of the following groups chosen by the candidate:—

GROUP I: C, D, F, A♭ majors; C, D, F, G♯ minors

GROUP II: C, D♭, F♯, G majors; C, C♯, F♯, G minors

(*a*) **Scales,** major and minor (*both* melodic *and* harmonic). Major scales of C, D♭ and D and minor scales of C, C♯ and D, three octaves; the other scales two octaves only.

(i) Separate bows, even notes, as example in Violin Grade VI;

(ii) Slurred, seven notes to a bow, as example in Violin Grade VI.

(*b*) **Arpeggios**—the major and minor common chords. Major and minor arpeggios of C, three octaves; the other arpeggios, two octaves only.

(i) Separate bows, even notes, as example in Violin Grade I;

(ii) Slurred, three notes to a bow, as example in Violin Grade IV.

(*c*) **Dominant Seventh** in the key of F (starting on the note C), two octaves; separate bows, even notes, as example in Violin Grade VI.

(*d*) **Chromatic Scales,** starting on C, D and E♭, two octaves; slurred bowing, four or six notes to a bow, at candidate's choice.

4. Playing at Sight.

5. Aural Tests for the Grade, see page 28.

Grade VII (Advanced)

1. Theory of Music, Grade V (Higher), must have been passed: see pages 12 and 21.

2. Four Works†:—

Either LIST A

Handel. First and second movements from Sonata in G minor, arr. Thurston Dart (*Schott 10114*)

Paul Hindemith. Meditation (The alternative lower line may be played) (*Schott*)

Campagnoli. No. 9 in B♭ *and* **No. 26 in A from Forty-one Caprices, Op. 22** (*Augener*)

or LIST B

Mozart. First movement from Sonata in E minor, K.304, arr. Watson Forbes (*Peters*)

Ibert. Aria (*United Music Publishers*)

Hoffmeister. No. 2 in A (Menuettino) *and* **No. 3 in F from Studies for Viola** (*Peters 1993*)

Selections may not be made from both lists, but as an alternative to the *second* piece in either list, the following may be chosen:—

Walter Piston. Interlude (*Boosey and Hawkes*)

3. Scales and Arpeggios, from memory, (*a*) and (*b*) in the keys specified in one of the following groups chosen by the candidate:—

GROUP I: C, D♭, E majors; C, C♯, E minors

GROUP II: D, E♭, F majors and minors

(*a*) **Scales,** major and minor (*both* melodic *and* harmonic), three octaves.
- (i) Separate bows, even notes, at a fairly quick pace, as example in Violin Grade VI;
- (ii) Slurred, seven notes to a bow, as example in Violin Grade VI.

(*b*) **Arpeggios**—the major and minor common chords, three octaves.
- (i) Separate bows, even notes, as example in Violin Grade I;
- (ii) Slurred, one bow ascending and one bow descending, as example in Violin Grade VII.

(*c*) **Dominant Sevenths,** Group I *or* Group II; i.e., the same group as already chosen for the scales and arpeggios; two octaves.

GROUP I: starting on C, D♭, E (keys of F, G♭, A)

GROUP II: starting on D, E♭, F (keys of G, A♭, B♭)
- (i) Separate bows, even notes, as example in Violin Grade VI.
- (ii) Slurred, even notes, four notes to a bow.

(*d*) **Chromatic Scales,** starting on the notes specified in the chosen group of scales and arpeggios, two octaves; slurred bowing, twelve notes to a bow.

---

† The music required for the Viola Examinations is NOT published by the Board, but may be obtained through a music seller.

4. Playing at Sight.

5. Aural Tests for the Grade, see pages 28 and 29.

Grade VIII (Final)

1. Theory of Music, Grade V (Higher), must have been passed: see pages 12 and 21.

2. Three Works†, one chosen by the candidate from each of the three groups A, B and C:—

GROUP A

1. **C. P. E. Bach-Casadesus. First movement from Concerto in D** (*Schirmer*)
2. **Brahms. Two Hungarian Dances, arr. Watson Forbes** (*Peters*)
3. **Norman Fulton. Introduction, Air and Reel** (*Oxford University Press*)

GROUP B

1. **Alan Richardson. First movement from Sonata** (*Augener*)
2. **Vitali. Ciaconna, arr. Louis Bailly** (*Schirmer*)
3. **Schubert. Sonata movement, arr. Watson Forbes** (*Augener*)

GROUP C

1. **Bach. First movement, Prelude, from Suite No. 2 in D minor** (*Six Suites for Viola, transcribed Watson Forbes. Chester*)
2. **Richard Arnell. No. 1, Bravura, and No. 2 Capriccio, from Partita** (*Hinrichsen*)
3. **Rode. No. 12 in C♯ minor of 24 Caprices** (*Peters*)

3. Scales and Arpeggios, from memory, in all the keys set in Grade VII (*both* groups), i.e. from C to F inclusive.

(*a*) **Scales,** major and minor
(*b*) **Arpeggios**
(*d*) **Chromatic Scales**
} Compass and bowing as in Grade VII

(*c*) **Dominant Sevenths,** two octaves, in the keys set in Grade VII, *both* groups: (i) separate bows, even notes; (ii) slurred, even notes, eight notes to a bow.

(*e*) **Scales in Double Notes,** one octave; E♭ major in thirds and in sixths, G major in octaves; separate bows.

4. Playing at Sight.

5. Aural Tests for the Grade, see page 29.

VIOLONCELLO

See page 46 for marks and for rules concerning accompaniment, tuning, fingering and playing at sight.

Grade I (Primary)

1. Three Works†:—

Either LIST A

Earnshaw. Melody. No. 2 of Seven Pieces, The Progressive Violoncellist (*Joseph Williams*)

Champ. Cavatina (*Augener*)

Whitehouse. Study in G. No. 5 of Progressive Studies (*Joseph Williams*)

or LIST B

Fitzenhagen. Ave Maria. No. 2, First Series of 30 Graded Pieces (*Augener*)

Doreen Carwithen. Rest in the Shade. No. 2 of Six Little Pieces, Set 2 (*Joseph Williams*)

Romberg. Study in C. No. 10 of Progressive Studies compiled Whitehouse (*Joseph Williams*)

Selections may not be made from both lists, but as an alternative to the *second* piece in either list, the following may be chosen:—

Niso Ticciati. Minuet. No. 7 of The Young Cellist, Vol. 1 (*Oxford University Press*)

2. Exercises: Set I of the 1963 edition for this Grade (*Associated Board*).

3. Scales and Arpeggios*, from memory:—

(*a*) **Major Scales** in the key of C (two octaves) and in the keys of G and D (one octave, starting on open strings); separate bows, as example in Violin Grade I.

Also the same scales, but with the quavers slurred two to a bow.

(*b*) **Arpeggios**—the major common chords of C, G and D (one octave, starting on open strings); separate bows only, as example in Violin Grade I.

4. Playing at Sight a melody in simple time in the major key of C, G or D. It will be put before the candidate to read through and play.

As an aid to the reading he may, but need not, first clap or tap the time-values of the notes while counting aloud the number of beats in each bar or giving the French time-names at the speed at which he will play it; and/or count aloud while playing the actual notes.

5. Aural Tests for the Grade, see page 26.

---

* Published by the Board.

† The music required for the Violoncello examinations, except the Exercises and Scales, Grades I to V, is NOT published by the Board, but may be obtained through a music seller.

Grade II (Elementary)

1. Three Works†:—

Either LIST A

Champ. Scherzino (*Augener*)
Tartini. Sarabanda. From Old Masters for Young Players (*Schott*)
Kummer. Study in D major No. 16 of Progressive Studies compiled Whitehouse (*Joseph Williams*)

or LIST B

Handel. March from Flavius. No. 6 of Easy Classics for the Cello, arr. Watson Forbes (*Oxford University Press*)
Buononcini. Rondeau. From Old Masters for Young Players (*Schott*)
Whitehouse. Study in G major. No. 17 of Progressive Studies (*Joseph Williams*)

Selections may not be made from both lists, but as an alternative to the *second* piece in either list, the following may be chosen:—

Beethoven. Ecossaise. No. 13 of Easy Classics, arr. Watson Forbes (*Oxford University Press*)

2. Exercises: Set I of the 1963 edition for this Grade (*Associated Board*).

3. Scales and Arpeggios*, from memory:—

(*a*) **Major Scales** in the keys of C, D and G (two octaves) and in B♭ (one octave) and the **Minor Scale** of G (harmonic *or* melodic at candidate's choice) (one octave).
- (i) Separate bows, as example in Violin Grade I;
- (ii) with the quavers slurred two to a bow.

(*b*) **Arpeggios**—the major common chords of C and D (two octaves) and of G and B♭ (one octave); separate bows, as example in Violin Grade I.

4. Playing at Sight.

5. Aural Tests for the Grade, see pages 26 and 27.

Grade III (Transitional)

1. Three Works†:—

Either LIST A

Handel. Chaconne. No. 9 of Easy Classics for the Cello, arr. Watson Forbes (*Oxford University Press*)
Telemann. Fanfare. No. 12 of Classical Pieces for the Beginner (*Schott 4918*)
Kummer. Study in C. No. 20 of Progressive Studies compiled Whitehouse (*Joseph Williams*)

or LIST B

Roy Thompson. Harlequin's Serenade. No. 2 of Three Frivolous Pieces (*Augener*)
Katharine Lovell. The Train. No. 2 of Three Summer Sketches (*Elkin*)
Whitehouse. Study in C. No. 23 of Progressive Studies (*Joseph Williams*)

Selections may not be made from both lists, but as an alternative to the *second* piece in either list, the following may be chosen:—

Niso Ticciati. Bourrée (unaccompanied). No. 3 of The Young Cellist, Vol. III. (Cello part available separately) (*Oxford University Press*)

2. Exercises: Set I of the 1963 edition for this Grade (*Associated Board*).

3. Scales and Arpeggios*, from memory:—

(*a*) **Major Scales** in the keys of D, E♭, F and G (two octaves) and **Minor Scales** (harmonic *or* melodic at candidate's choice) in the keys of C, G and D (one octave, starting on open strings).

(i) Separate bows, as example in Violin Grade I;

(ii) with the quavers slurred two to a bow.

(*b*) **Arpeggios**—the common chords of D major (two octaves), of E♭, F and G majors (one octave, the lowest) and of C, G and D minors (one octave, starting on open strings); separate bows as example in Violin Grade I.

4. Playing at Sight.

5. Aural Tests for the Grade, see page 27.

Grade IV (Lower)

1. Three Works†:—

Either LIST A

Earnshaw. Tarantelle, Op. 44, No. 4 (*Joseph Williams*)
Franck. Air Varié, arr. Lloyd Webber (*Weekes*)
Lee. Study in D major. No. 26 of Progressive Studies compiled Whitehouse (*Joseph Williams*)

or LIST B

George Dyson. Intermezzo from Six Lyric Pieces (*Stainer and Bell*)
Cedric Sharpe. Chansonnette. No. 5 of Five Little Solos (*Joseph Williams*)
Dotzauer. No. 8 in E minor of 40 Studies (*Augener 7771*)

Selections may not be made from both lists, but as an alternative to the *second* piece in either list, the following may be chosen:—

Howard Ferguson. A Hushaby from Five Irish Folk Tunes (*Oxford University Press*)

2. Exercises: Set I of the 1963 edition for this Grade (*Associated Board*).

3. Scales and Arpeggios*, from memory, in the following keys:—
D♭, E♭, A majors; D, G minors

(*a*) **Scales,** major and minor (harmonic *or* melodic at candidate's choice) (two octaves).

(i) Separate bows, as example in Violin Grade I;

(ii) Slurred, two beats to a bow, as example in Violin Grade IV.

(*b*) **Arpeggios**—the major and minor common chords.

(i) Separate bows, as example in Violin Grade I (two octaves);

(ii) Slurred, three notes to a bow, as example in Violin Grade IV.

4. Playing at Sight.

5. Aural Tests for the Grade, see page 27.

---

* Published by the Board.

† The music required for the Violoncello examinations, except the Exercises and Scales, Grades I to V, is NOT published by the Board, but may be obtained through a music seller.

Grade V (Higher)

1. Three Works†:—

Either LIST A

Rubino. Adagio *and* **Haydn. Allegro** } **from Lost Melodies, ed. Stutschewsky** (*Universal 10627*)
Dotzauer. No. 5 in C of 40 Studies (*Augener 7771*)

or LIST B

Corelli. Adagio from Sonata, Op. 5, No. 1 (*Peters 4211*)
Squire. Joyeuse. No. 11 of 30 Graded Pieces (*Augener*)
Dotzauer. No. 6 in A minor of 40 Studies (*Augener 7771*)

Selections may not be made from both lists, but as an alternative to the *second* piece in either list, the following may be chosen:—

Handel. Menuet in F (without the up-bow staccato). No. 6 of Selected Pieces, arr. Burmester—van Lier (*Harris*)

2. Exercises: Set I of the 1963 edition for this Grade (*Associated Board*).

3. Scales and Arpeggios*, from memory, in the following keys:—

D♭, E, A♭, B♭ majors; C, E minors

(*a*) **Scales,** major and minor (harmonic *or* melodic at candidate's choice) (two octaves).
 (i) Separate bows, as example in Violin Grade I;
 (ii) Slurred, two beats to a bow, as example in Violin Grade IV.

(*b*) **Arpeggios**—the major and minor common chords (two octaves).
 (i) Separate bows, as example in Violin Grade I;
 (ii) Slurred, three notes to a bow, as example in Violin Grade IV.

(*c*) **Chromatic Scales** starting on open strings C, G and D (one octave); separate bows.

4. Playing at Sight.

5. Aural Tests for the Grade, see pages 27 and 28.

Grade VI (Intermediate)

1. Theory of Music, Grade V (Higher), must have been passed: see pages 12 and 21.

2. Four Works†:—

Either LIST A

Philidor. La Sauterelle from Lost Melodies ed. Stutschewsky (*Universal 10627*)
Grieg. Air from The Holberg Suite, arr. Watson Forbes (*Oxford University Press*)
Dotzauer. No. 32 in E minor and No. 33 in G of 40 Studies (*Augener 7771*)

(*continued*)

or LIST B

Trowell. Roundelay, Op. 11, No. 2 (*Schott*)
DeFesch. Siciliano and Allemanda from Sonata in D minor, arr. Moffat (*Schott*)
Dotzauer. No. 25 in G minor and No. 24 in B♭ of 40 Studies (*Augener 7771*)

Selections may not be made from both lists, but as an alternative to the *second* piece in either list, the following may be chosen:—

Duport. No. 2 of Two Melodies, arr. Benoy and Burrowes (*Oxford University Press*)

3. Scales and Arpeggios, from memory; (*a*) and (*b*) in the keys specified in one of the following groups chosen by the candidate:—

GROUP I: C, E, A♭ majors; C, E, G♯ minors
GROUP II: D♭, F, A majors; C♯, F, A minors
GROUP III: D, F♯, B♭ majors and minors
GROUP IV: E♭, G, B majors and minors

(*a*) **Scales,** major and minor (*both* melodic *and* harmonic).
(i) Separate bows, even notes, as example in Violin Grade VI;
(ii) Slurred, seven notes to a bow, as example in Violin Grade VI.

Major scales of C, D♭, D, E♭ and minor scales of C, C♯, D and E♭, three octaves; the other scales two octaves only.

(*b*) **Arpeggios**—the major and minor common chords, two octaves.
(i) Separate bows, even notes, as example in Violin Grade I;
(ii) Slurred, three notes to a bow, as example in Violin Grade IV.

(*c*) **Dominant Seventh** in the key of F, starting on the note C, two octaves; separate bows, even notes, as example in Violin Grade VI.

(*d*) **Chromatic Scales** starting on C, C♯ and D, two octaves; slurred bowing, four or six notes to a bow, at candidate's choice.

4. Playing at Sight.

5. Aural Tests for the Grade, see page 28.

Grade VII (Advanced)

1. Theory of Music, Grade V (Higher), must have been passed: see pages 12 and 21.

2. Four Works†:—

Either LIST A

Popper. Arlequin, Op. 3, No. 1 (*Augener*)
Armstrong Gibbs. Nocturne, Op. 121, No. 2 (*Augener*)
Dotzauer. No. 34 in D (one bow to a bar) and No. 38 in A minor of 40 Studies (*Augener 7771*)

---

† The music required for the Violoncello examinations is NOT published by the Board, but may be obtained through a music seller.

or LIST B

Couperin. La Tromba and Air de Diable, from Pièces en Concert, ed. Bazelaire (*United Music Publishers*)
Frederic Austin. Captain Cockchafer (*Selected Series No. 39. Schott*)
Dotzauer. No. 28 in G minor and No. 36 in G minor of 40 Studies (*Augener 7771*)

Selections may not be made from both lists, but as an alternative to the *second* piece in either list, the following may be chosen:—

Saint-Saëns. The Swan. (*United Music Publishers*)

3. **Scales and Arpeggios,** from memory: (*a*) and (*b*) in the keys specified in one of the following groups chosen by the candidate:—

GROUP I: C, E♭, F♯, A majors and minors
GROUP II: D♭, E, G, B♭ majors; C♯, E, G, B♭ minors
GROUP III: D, F, A♭, B majors; D, F, G♯, B minors

(*a*) **Scales,** major and minor (*both* melodic *and* harmonic), three octaves.
(i) Separate bows, even notes, at a fairly quick pace, as example in Violin Grade VI;
(ii) Slurred, seven notes to a bow, as example in Violin Grade VI.

(*b*) **Arpeggios**—the major and minor common chords.
(i) Separate bows, as example in Violin Grade I;
(ii) Slurred, one bow ascending and one bow descending, as example in Violin Grade VII.

Major arpeggios of C, D♭ and D, three octaves; the other arpeggios two octaves only.

(*c*) **Dominant Sevenths,** Group I, *or* Group II *or* Group III; i.e., the same group as already chosen for the scales and arpeggios; two octaves.

GROUP I: starting on C, E♭, F♯, A (keys of F, A♭, B, D)
GROUP II: starting on D♭, E, G, B♭ (keys of G♭, A, C, E♭)
GROUP III: starting on D, F, A♭, B (keys of G, B♭, D♭, E)

(i) Separate bows, even notes, as example in Violin Grade VI;
(ii) Slurred, even notes, four notes to a bow.

(*d*) **Chromatic Scales,** starting on the notes specified in the chosen group for scales and arpeggios, two octaves; slurred bowing, twelve notes to a bow.

4. **Playing at Sight.**

5. **Aural Tests** for the Grade, see pages 28 and 29.

Grade VIII (Final)

1. Theory of Music, Grade V (Higher), must have been passed: see pages 12 and 21.

2. Three Works†, one chosen by the candidate from each of the three groups A, B and C:—

GROUP A

1. **Bach.** *Andante* **and** *Allegro Moderato* **from Gamba Sonata in G major** (*Peters*)
2. **Dohnanyi. Tema and Variazioni from Sonata in B♭ minor, Op. 8** (*Schott*)
3. **Leonardo Leo. Concerto in D, arr. Cilea. First and second movements,** *Andantino grazioso* and *Larghetto con poco moto*. (*Ricordi*)
4. **Max Bruch. Kol Nidrei** (*Simrock-Lengnick*)

GROUP B

1. **Boccherini. Rondo, arr. Bazelaire** (*United Music Publishers*)
2. **Samuel Barber. Sonata for Violoncello and Piano. Third movement** (*Schirmer-Chappell*)
3. **Hurlstone. Rondo from Sonata in D** (*Curwen*)
4. **Benjamin Frankel. Nos. 2 and 3 of Three Poems, Op. 23** (*Augener*)

GROUP C

1. **Elisabeth Lutyens. Prelude and Capriccio, Op. 20** (*Mills Music*)
2. **Bach. Prelude and Courante from Suite No. 3 in C**
3. **Franchomme. Caprice No. 10 in E♭, Op. 7** (*Augener*)
4. **Popper. Study No. 5 from High School, Op. 73, Book I** (*Novello*)

3. Scales and Arpeggios, from memory; (*a*) and (*b*) in the keys specified in one of the following groups chosen by the candidate:—

GROUP I: C, E, F, A♭ majors; C, E, F, G♯ minors

GROUP II: D♭, E♭, F♯, A majors; C♯, E♭, F♯, A minors

(*a*) **Scales,** major and minor (three octaves), in the same forms as set for Grade VII.

(*b*) **Arpeggios**—the major and minor common chords (three octaves).

(i) Separate bows, as example in Violin Grade I;

(ii) Slurred; A♭ and A majors and G♯ and A minors three notes to a bow; the other arpeggios, one bow ascending and one bow descending, as example in Violin Grade VII.

(*c*) **Dominant Sevenths,** Group I *or* Group II; i.e., the same group as already chosen for the scales and arpeggios (two octaves).

GROUP I: starting on C, E, F, A♭ (keys of F, A, B♭, D♭)

GROUP II: starting on D♭, E♭, F♯, A (keys of G♭, A♭, B, D)

(i) Separate bows, even notes, as example in Violin Grade VI;

(ii) Slurred, even notes, one bow ascending and one bow descending.

(*d*) **Chromatic Scales,** starting on any note from C to G inclusive, slurred, twelve notes to a bow (two octaves).

4. Playing at Sight.

5. Aural Tests for the Grade, see page 29.

---

† The music required for the Violoncello examinations is NOT published by the Board, but may be obtained through a music seller.

SINGING

Grades IV (Lower) to VIII (Final) only

The Board refrains from offering to examine candidates in Solo Singing below Grade IV, being of the opinion that below this stage young voices should be allowed to develop without the strain of solo singing before examiners. There are examinations in Class Singing in the early grades for which a separate syllabus can be obtained on application.

Schedule of maximum marks:—

Grades	IV-VI	VII	VIII
Songs—			
1	42	48	42
2	42	36	27
3	—	—	27
Technical Exercises	30	30	18
Singing at Sight	18	18	18
Aural Tests	18	18	18
Total	150	150	150

Purity of vowels and tone production, breath control, flexibility, intonation, articulation and memory will all be taken into account in the marking.

In Grades IV to VII at least one, and in Grade VIII at least two, of the songs must be sung from memory.

For the Songs and Recitatives, candidates must **provide their own accompanists** who may remain in the room only while so engaged. Their teachers may act as accompanists, but the Examiner will not do so except in the Sight Singing test.

The Technical Exercises will be sung unaccompanied.

The Sight Singing will be sung without words on any vowel or to sol-fa as the candidate prefers.

The Examiner will take into consideration the care and discretion used in choosing songs from the different lists so as to display variety and contrast of style and mood. The songs specified in the lists given below for each Grade may be sung in any published key appropriate to the compass of the candidate's voice. Where keys are indicated, they are given merely as a guide and are not obligatory. Candidates may use any edition, see Regulation 21(*a*).

All songs with foreign words which have an English translation may be sung in English. Extended trills in the songs may be omitted.

The Candidate should bring a copy of each of his songs for the accompanist's use, and, except for those sung from memory, a separate copy for himself.

Grade IV (Lower)

1. Two songs, both from the lists for the same voice, one from List A and one from List B, at the candidate's choice. One at least of the songs must be sung from memory.

Soprano and Mezzo Soprano

LIST A

1. **Mendelssohn. I will sing of Thy great mercies (St. Paul)** (*Novello S.S. 922*)
2. **Arne. Where the bee sucks**
3. **Purcell. Nymphs and Shepherds** (*F, G—Cramer*)

LIST B

1. **Lennox Berkeley. The Thresher** (*O.U.P.*)
2. **O Waly, Waly, arr. Cecil Sharp** (*Novello*)
3. **Hugh Roberton. Maureen** (*E♭, F—Paterson*)

Contralto and Mezzo Contralto

LIST A

1. **Dunhill. How soft upon the evening air** (*G—Curwen 72096*)
2. **Handel. Verdi Prati (Verdant Meadows)** (*Ascherberg S.S. 28*)
3. **Traditional. Early one morning**

LIST B

1. **Stanford. A soft day** (*D♭—Stainer and Bell*)
2. **Somervell. Shepherd's Cradle Song** (*E♭, F—Ashdown*)
3. **Max Reger. The Golden Bird. No. 2 of Two Cradle Songs** (*Medium voice—Ascherberg*)

Tenor

LIST A

1. **An Eriskay Love-lilt, arr. Kennedy Fraser** (*A—Boosey and Hawkes*)
2. **Handel. Silent Worship** (*A—Curwen*)
3. **The crystal Spring, arr. Cecil Sharp** (*Novello S.S. 952*)

LIST B

1. **Schubert. Who is Sylvia?** (*A—Paxton*)
2. **Michael Head. Sweet chance that led my steps** (*High key—Boosey and Hawkes*)
3. **Quilter. O mistress mine** (*G—Boosey and Hawkes*)

Baritone and Bass

LIST A

1. **Once I loved a Maiden fair, arr. Somervell** (*G—Cramer*)
2. **The Jolly Plough Boy, arr. Vaughan Williams** (*Novello S.S. 1128*)
3. **As I walked through the meadows, arr. Cecil Sharp** (*Novello S.S. 950*)

LIST B

1. **Beethoven. Ich liebe dich (I love you)** (*E♭—Elkin*)
2. **Schubert. An die Laute (The Cither)** (*D—Augener*)
3. **Ford. Since first I saw your face** (*D—Stainer and Bell*)
4. **Eric H. Thiman. The silver birch** (*C—Curwen*)

2. Technical Exercises, as published by the Board for this Grade in 1962.

3. Singing at sight, with a simple accompaniment played by the Examiner.

4. Aural Tests of the standard set for Grade II in other subjects (see pages 26 and 27).

Grade V (Higher)

1. Two Songs, both from the lists for the same voice, one from List A and one from List B, at the candidate's choice. One at least of the songs must be sung from memory.

Soprano and Mezzo Soprano

LIST A

1. **Hook. Hail, lovely rose, arr. Ella Ivimey** (*Augener*)
2. **Campra. Charmant Papillon (Brilliant butterfly)** (*Augener*)
3. **Diack. Little Polly Flinders** (*E♭, F—Paterson*)

LIST B

1. **Go from my window, go, arr. Somervell** (*A♭, B♭—Cramer*)
3. **Michael Head. When sweet Ann sings** (*E♭, F—Boosey and Hawkes*)
3. **Edmund Rubbra. Hymn to the Virgin** (*Lengnick*)

Contralto and Mezzo Contralto

LIST A

1. **Purcell. I attempt from love's sickness to fly** (*F—Hundred Best Songs, Vol. IV, Paterson*)
2. **Rosseter. When Laura smiles** (*Low key—Stainer and Bell*)
3. **Maurice Blower. Music with her silver sound** (*Elkin*)

LIST B

1. **Mary Plumstead. My true love hath my heart** (*Elkin*)
2. **Roger Quilter. Fairy Lullaby** (*F, A♭—Chappell*)
3. **Schubert. An die Musik (To Music)** (*B♭, B—Augener*)

Tenor

LIST A

1. **Purcell. I attempt from love's sickness to fly** (*A♭—Ascherberg*)
2. **Pilkington. Down a down thus Phyllis sung** (*High voice, Book III of Forty Elizabethan Songs—Stainer and Bell*)
3. **Anon. Have you seen but a white lily grow, arr. Warlock** (*O.U.P.*)

LIST B

1. **German. The English Rose (Merrie England)** (*B♭—Chappell*)
2. **Quilter. The Fuschia Tree** (*C♯ minor—Boosey and Hawkes*)
3. **Frank Bridge. Go not, happy day** (*A—Boosey and Hawkes*)

Baritone and Bass

LIST A

1. **Mozart. Deh! vieni alla finestra (Don Giovanni)** (*Augener*)
2. **Martini. Plaisir d'amour** (*F—Augener*)
3. **Lully. Bois épais (Forest dim)** (*E♭—Augener*)
4. **Over the mountains, arr. Quilter** (*G—Boosey and Hawkes*)

LIST B

1. **German. The Yeoman of England (Merrie England)** (*D—Chappell*)
2. **Martin Shaw. I know a bank** (*F—Cramer*)
3. **Edwin Benbow. In youth is pleasure** (*E♭—Cramer*)
4. **John Ireland. If there were dreams to sell** (*D♭—Boosey and Hawkes*)

2. Technical Exercises, as published by the Board for this Grade in 1962.

3. Singing at sight, with a simple accompaniment played by the Examiner.

4. Aural Tests of the standard set for Grade III in other subjects (see page 27).

Grade VI (Intermediate)

1. Theory of Music, Grade V (Higher), must have been passed: see pages 12 and 21.

2. Two Songs, both from the lists for the same voice, one from List A and one from List B, at the candidate's choice. One at least of the songs must be sung from memory.

Soprano and Mezzo Soprano

LIST A

1. **Spohr. Rose softly blooming** (*B♭, G—Ascherberg*)
2. **Gounod. Faites-lui mes aveux (The Flower Song) (Faust)** (*B♭—Chappell*)
3. **Handel. Let me wander not unseen (L'Allegro)** (*Novello S.S. 1915*)

LIST B

1. **Eric Coates. Any one of Four Old English Songs** (*Medium or high voice—Boosey and Hawkes*)
2. **Storace. The summer heats bestowing, arr. Ella Ivimey** (*Augener*)
3. **Armstrong Gibbs. Silver** (*F♯ minor—Boosey and Hawkes*)

Contralto and Mezzo Contralto

LIST A

1. **Haydn. The mermaid's song** (*Augener*)
2. **Handel. On the valleys, dark and cheerless** (*Secular Solos, Contralto—Novello*)
3. **Purcell. Music for awhile** (*G minor—Ashdown; F minor—Paxton*)

LIST B

1. **Merikanto. A fairy tale by the fire** (*Chester*)
2. **Winifred Bury. I know a bank** (*E♭—Paterson*)
3. **Graham Peel. Gipsies** (*D♭—Chappell*)
4. **Cyril Scott. Lullaby** (*D♭—Elkin*)

Tenor

LIST A

1. **Handel. Love in her eyes sits playing (Acis and Galatea)** (*Novello*)
2. **Sullivan. Take a pair of sparkling eyes (The Gondoliers)** (*F—Chappell*)
3. **The gentle maiden, arr. Somervell** (*F—Cramer*)

LIST B

1. **Elgar. The shepherd's song** (*F—Ascherberg*)
2. **Schubert. Der Musensohn (Wandering Minstrel)** (*G—Augener*)
3. **Ernest Farrar. Brittany** (*G—Novello*)

Baritone and Bass

LIST A

1. **The Hostel, arr. Bairstow** (*D—Stainer and Bell*)
2. **Arne. Now Phoebus sinketh in the west** (*E♭—Paxton*)
3. **Handel. Droop not young lover** (*Cramer*)
4. **Mendelssohn. For the mountains shall depart (Elijah)** (*Novello*)

LIST B

1. **Michael Head. Mamble** (*B♭—Boosey and Hawkes*)
2. **Grieg. A Swan** (*E♭, F—Hinrichsen*)
3. **Boughton. The Old Bard's Song** (*The Immortal Hour*) (*G minor—Stainer and Bell*)
4. **Stanley Taylor. The Passionate Shepherd to his Love** (*E—Cramer*)

3. Technical Exercises, as published by the Board for this Grade in 1962.

4. Singing at sight, with a simple accompaniment played by the Examiner.

5. Aural Tests of the standard set for Grade IV in other subjects (see page 27).

Grade VII (Advanced)

1. Theory of Music, Grade V (Higher), must have been passed: see pages 12 and 21.

2. A Recitative and Aria from List A, and a **Song** from List B, chosen by the candidate from lists for the same voice. One at least of the songs must be sung from memory.

Soprano and Mezzo Soprano

LIST A

1. **Handel. Recit.: Hold not these black illusions**
Aria: The smiling dawn of happy day } **(Jephtha)** (*Augener*)

2. **Bach. Recit.: Although our eyes**
Aria: Jesus Saviour, I am Thine } **Nos. 18 and 19 St. Matthew Passion** (*Novello*)

3. **Handel. Recit.: My Jonathan**
Aria: Subtle love } **(Alexander Balus)** (*A—Ascherberg S.S. 59*)

4. **Mozart. Recit.: Giunse alfin il momento**
Aria: Deh vieni non tardar } (*Soprano Songs from Figaro, Book 2, Novello*)

LIST B

1. **Warlock. The first mercy** (*Boosey and Hawkes*)

2. **Montague Phillips. Sail my ships (Rebel Maid)** (*Chappell*)

3. **Delius. Sweet Venevil** (*O.U.P.*)

4. **Samuel Barber. Sure on this shining night** (*B♭—Schirmer*)

Contralto and Mezzo Contralto

LIST A

1. **Handel. Recit.: With might endued**
Aria: The Holy One of Israel } **(Samson)** (*Complete score only—Novello*)

2. **Mozart. Recit.: A questo seno (Unto my bosom)**
Aria: Quando miro quel bel ciglio (As upon thy lovely features) } (*C or D♭ Ascherberg S.S. 16*)

3. **Handel. Recit.: Horror! Confusion!**
Aria: Fury, with red sparkling eyes } **(Alexander Balus)** (*Ascherberg S.S. 58*)

4. **Gluck. Recit. and Aria: Che Faro (Orfeo)** (*Ricordi*)

LIST B

1. **Sigurd Lie. Soft-footed snow** (*C minor, D minor—Lengnick*)

2. **Vaughan Williams. The sky above the roof** (*Boosey and Hawkes*)

3. **Eric H. Thiman. Flower of Heaven** (*E♭—Elkin*)

4. **German. O peaceful England (Merrie England)** (*Chappell*)

(*continued*)

Tenor

LIST A

1. **Mendelssohn. Recit.: Ye people rend your hearts**
Aria: If with all your hearts } **(Elijah)** ***(Novello)***

2. **Handel. Recit.: See she appears**
Aria: Where'er you walk } **(Semele)** ***(Ascherberg S.S. 42)***

3. **Haydn. Recit.: And God created man**
Aria: In native worth } **(The Creation)** ***(Novello)***

LIST B

1. **Hageman. Do not go, my love (*F♯ minor—Chappell*)**

2. **Warlock. Milkmaids (*G—Ashdown*)**

3. **Brahms. Minnelied (Love Song) (*B♭, D—Lengnick*)**

Baritone and Bass

LIST A

1. **Handel. Recit.: I feel the Deity within**
Aria: Arm, arm, ye brave } **(Judas Maccabbaeus)** ***(Augener)***

2. **Haydn. Recit.: At last from Aries**
Aria: With joy the impatient husbandman } **(The Seasons) (Spring)** ***(Full score only—Novello)***

3. **Handel. Recit.: From the rage of the tempest**
Aria: Hear me! Ye winds and waves } **(Scipio)** ***(G minor—Boosey and Hawkes)***

4. **Wagner. Recit.: Wie Todesahnung (Like death's dark shadow)**
Aria: O du, mein holder Abendstern (O star of Eve) } **(Tannhäuser)** ***(Augener)***

LIST B

1. **Schumann. Dein Angesicht (Thy face) (*C—Cramer*)**

2. **Vaughan Williams. The Vagabond (*C minor—Boosey and Hawkes*)**

3. **Stanford. The bold unbiddable child (*C minor, D minor—Stainer and Bell*)**

4. **Butterworth. Is my team ploughing? (*B♭—Augener*)**

3. Technical Exercises, as published by the Board for this Grade in 1962.

4. Singing at sight, with a simple accompaniment played by the Examiner.

5. Aural Tests of the standard set for Grade V in other subjects (see pages 27 and 28).

Grade VIII (Final)

1. Theory of Music, Grade V (Higher), must have been passed: see pages 12 and 21.

2. A Recitative and Aria from List A and **Two Songs,** one from List B and one from List C, all from Lists for the same voice, at the candidate's choice. Two at least of the songs must be sung from memory.

Soprano and Mezzo Soprano

LIST A

1. **Handel. Recit.: Ne' trionfi d'Alessandro (Alexander's) course of glory)**
Aria: Lusinghe più care (Ye cupids and graces) } **(Alessandro)** (*Augener*)
2. **Bizet. Recit. and Aria: Cavatina de Leila (Les Pêcheurs de Perles) (Cadenza may be omitted)** (*F—U.M.P.*)
3. **Handel. Recit.: 'Tis done**
Aria: Heart, the seat of soft delight } **(Acis and Galatea)** (*Novello*)
4. **Sullivan. Recit: 'Tis done, I am a bride**
Aria: E'er half an hour has rung } **(Yeoman of the Guard)** (*Full score only—Chappell*)
5. **Mozart. Recit.: Solitudini amiche (Friendly solitude)**
Aria: Zeffiretti lusinghieri (Gentle Zephyr) } **(Idomeneo)** (*Ascherberg S.O. 85*)

LIST B

1. **Brahms. An die Nachtigall (To the nightingale)** (*D, E—Lengnick*)
2. **Mahler. Wo die schönen Trompeten blasen** (*Universal 3647A*)
3. **Schumann. Der Nussbaum (The nut tree)** (*G—Augener*)
4. **Fauré. Après un Rêve** (*Top Key—United Music Publishers*)

LIST C

1. **Herbert Howells. Gavotte** (*O.U.P.*)
2. **Vaughan Williams. Here on my throne (Hugh the Drover)** (*Curwen*)
3. **Parry. My heart is like a singing bird** (*Novello*)
4. **Delius. The homeward way** (*O.U.P.*)
5. **Michael Head. On the wings of the wind** (*Boosey and Hawkes*)

Contralto and Mezzo Contralto

LIST A

1. **Handel. Recit.: Gold now is common**
Aria: How green our fertile pastures } **(Solomon)** (*Full score—Novello*) (*also in Handel's Songs, ed. Ford, Vol. 4—Boosey*)
2. **Bach. Recit.: See now the bridegroom**
Aria: Prepare thyself, Zion } **(Nos. 3 and 4, Christmas Oratorio, Part I)** (*Novello*)
3. **Massenet. Recit.: Celui dont les paroles**
Aria: Il est doux, il est bon } **(Herodiade)** (*C—only published in French—U.M.P.*
4. **Handel. Recit.: 'Twill be a painful separation**
Aria: In gentle murmurs } **(Jephtha)** (*E minor—Augener*)

LIST B

1. **Brahms. Wie Melodien zieht es mir (Sweet Melodies), Op. 105, No. 1** (*A—Lengnick*)
2. **Gluck. O del mio dolce ardor (O Zephyr soft and kind) (Paride ed Elena)** (*D, E minor—Ascherberg S.S. 12*)
3. **Richard Strauss. Allerseelen (All Souls' Day)** (*B—Universal*)
4. **Debussy. Romance.** (*Low voice—U.M.P.*)
5. **Respighi. Nebbie (Mists)** (*Low voice—Ricordi*)

(*continued*)

LIST C

1. **Hageman. Music I heard with you** (*Low voice—Elkin*)
2. **Herbert Howells. King David** (*Boosey and Hawkes*)
3. **Michael Head. Ave Maria** (*Boosey and Hawkes*)
4. **Arnold Bax. Cradle Song** (*Chappell*)
5. **Stanford. The Fairy Lough** (*D—Boosey and Hawkes*)

Tenor

LIST A

1. **Handel. Recit.: Thanks to my brethren / Aria: How vain is man (Judas Maccabbaeus)** (*Augener*)
2. **Bach. Recit.: Today the highest / Aria: Ten thousand times thousand (Cantata No. 43)** (*Novello*)
3. **Mozart. Recit.: Come mai creder deggio (I can scarce comprehend it) / Aria: Dalla sua pace (All joy and pleasure) (Don Giovanni)** (*Paxton*)

LIST B

1. **Schubert. Der Neugierige (The questioner)** (*B—Augener*)
2. **Beethoven. Adelaide** (*B♭—Augener*)
3. **Fauré. Clair de lune** (*C minor—U.M.P.*)

LIST C

1. **Yarmouth Fair, arr. Warlock.** (*O.U.P.*)
2. **Frank Bridge. E'en as a lovely flower** (*G—Boosey and Hawkes*)
3. **John Ireland. Goal and Wicket** (*E minor—Augener*)

Baritone and Bass

LIST A

1. **Handel. Recit.: Behold, I tell you a mystery / Aria: The trumpet shall sound (Messiah) (omit 2nd section)** (*Novello*)
2. **Purcell. Recit. and Aria: Ye twice ten hundred Deities** (*Augener*)
3. **Bach. Recit.: Perhaps you're right / Aria: Good fellows be merry (Peasant Cantata) (Cut from ⊕ to ⊕ in middle section.)** (*Paterson*)
4. **Haydn. Recit.: And God said, Let the waters / Aria: Rolling in foaming billows (The Creation)** (*Novello*)

LIST B

1. **Parry. Love is a bable** (*Novello*)
2. **Schubert. Aufenthalt (Resting Place)** (*Low Key—Augener*)
3. **Schumann. Die beiden Grenadiere (The Two Grenadiers)** (*G mi—Augener*)
4. **Wolf. Anakreons Grab (Anacreon's Grave)** (*D—Peters*)

LIST C

1. **Charles Wood. Ethiopia saluting the Colours** (*A♭—Boosey and Hawkes*)
2. **Finzi. Come away, death** (*B minor—Boosey and Hawkes*)
3. **Stanford. The Pibroch** (*B minor—Ashdown*)
4. **Korbay. Mohács Field** (*B—Schott*)

3. Technical Exercises, as published by the Board for this Grade in 1962.

4. Singing at sight, with a simple accompaniment played by the Examiner.

5. Aural Tests of the standard set for Grade VI in other subjects (see page 28).

GENERAL MUSICIANSHIP

Grades IV (Lower) to VII (Advanced) only

These examinations are designed to widen the general musical understanding of candidates. Some of the tests involve reproduction from memory and these can be prepared; others will be answered impromptu. Although they are not intended to be tests in piano playing as such, their performance clearly presupposes a certain keyboard facility.

The examination may last about 15 minutes in Grades IV and V, 20 minutes in Grade VI and 25 minutes in Grade VII.

Schedule of maximum marks:—

	Grade	IV	V & VI	VII
Keyboard Tests (i)	.. ..	30	15	12
(ii)	.. ..	21	15	24
(iii)	.. ..	24	24	21
(iv)	.. ..	27	24	24
(v)	.. ..	—	24	21
Sight Singing or Playing	..	24	24	24
Aural Tests	.. .. ..	24	24	24
		150	150	150

Candidates must be prepared:—

Grade IV (Lower)

1. Keyboard Tests

(i) In the major keys of C, G, D, F and B♭:—

(*a*) To play single isolated chords of tonic, dominant and subdominant in four-part harmony (three notes in the R.H. and one in the L.H.).

(*b*) To play the key-chord and a cadential progression forming a perfect or a plagal cadence in four-part harmony (three notes in the R.H. and one in the L.H.).

Examples:

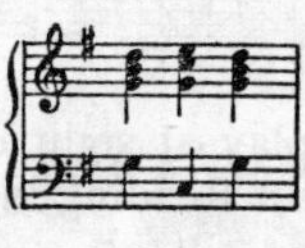

Candidates are not obliged to reproduce the lay-out of the chords in these examples. Any satisfactory spacing will be accepted.

(*c*) To play from a printed copy a four-bar melody, harmonising the last two notes to form a perfect or a plagal cadence.

Example: 

(ii) To play a piece or section of a piece, not less than 16 bars in length, previously chosen by the candidate from any Grade I Album of Pianoforte pieces published by the Board*, and then to transpose it into any key chosen by the candidate, at least a whole tone higher or lower than the original.

(iii) To transpose at sight from a printed copy a diatonic melody of about eight bars written in the major key of C, G or F into a key a tone higher or lower. The candidate may play the melody twice in the original key.

Example: 

(iv) To play from a printed copy a four-bar phrase in simple time written in the major key of C, G or F, and then to continue by adding an answering four-bar phrase.

Example: 

2. Sight Singing or Sight Playing (at candidate's choice)

Either: To sing at sight a simple diatonic melody in the major key of C, G, D, F or B♭ or in the minor key of A, E, B, D or G. The key-chord and first note will be sounded by the Examiner.

Example: 

Or: To play at sight on the pianoforte a test of similar difficulty to the Sight Reading in Pianoforte Grade III.

* The candidate must bring his own copy. This piece may be taken from a book of examination pieces, past or present, or from any of the permanent graded albums.

3. Aural Tests

(i) To recognise cadential progressions (perfect or plagal) in major keys. The key-chord will be sounded and followed immediately by the two chords forming the progression played twice by the Examiner.

(ii) To recognise whether the key of a melody played by the Examiner is major or minor.

(iii) To sing or play from memory the lower part of a two-part passage consisting of not more than three successive intervals played twice by the Examiner. The key-chord will first be sounded.

Examples: 

(iv) To clap the rhythm-pattern of a melody played twice by the Examiner; to say whether the time is duple, triple or quadruple; and to beat time when the music is repeated by the Examiner.

(v) To sing or play from memory a melodic phrase of about seven notes played twice by the Examiner. The key-chord will first be sounded.

Examples: 

Grade V (Higher)

1. Keyboard Tests

(i) To play perfect, plagal or imperfect (I-V) cadential progressions in four-part harmony (three parts in the R.H. and one in the L.H.) or in any free style, at the candidate's choice, in the major keys of C, G, D, F or B♭ and in the minor keys of A, E or D.

(ii) To play a piece or section of a piece* not less than 16 bars in length previously chosen by the candidate from any Grade II album of Pianoforte pieces published by the Board and then to transpose it into any key at least a whole tone higher or lower than the original. The new key is to be chosen by the candidate.

(iii) To harmonise at sight a very simple diatonic melody in the key of C major. The melody will be in 2/4 or 3/4 time; it can and may be harmonised by chords chosen from the tonic, dominant, subdominant or supertonic in root position, but the candidate need not be limited to using these chords. The candidate may play the melody twice before harmonising it.

Example: 

(iv) To transpose at sight from a printed copy a very simple diatonic piece in two parts, written on the treble and bass staves, about eight bars in length in the key of C, G or F major into a key a tone higher or lower. The candidate may play the test twice in the original key.

Example: 

(v) To play from a printed copy a four-bar phrase in simple time written in the key of C major, and then to continue by adding an answering melodic phrase modulating to the dominant.

Example: 

2. Sight Singing or Sight Playing (at candidate's choice)

Either: To sing at sight a diatonic melody in the major key of C, G, D, F or B♭ or in the minor key of A, E, B, D or G. The key-chord and first note will be sounded by the Examiner.

Examples: 

or

Or: To play at sight on the pianoforte a test of similar difficulty to the Sight Reading in Pianoforte Grade IV.

3. Aural Tests

(i) To recognise perfect, plagal and imperfect (I-V) cadential progressions in major and minor keys. The key-chord will be sounded and followed immediately by the two chords forming the progression, played twice by the Examiner.

(ii) To sing or play from memory the lower part of a two-part phrase consisting of not more than four successive intervals played twice by the Examiner. The key-chord will first be sounded.

Examples:

(iii) (*a*) To clap the rhythm-pattern of a melody played twice by the Examiner; to say whether the time is simple duple, triple or quadruple; and to beat time when the music is repeated by the Examiner.

(*b*) To identify note values (e.g., as minim, crotchet, quaver, including dotted notes) of a simple two-bar phrase in 2/4 or 3/4 time, the second bar of which will consist of one sound. The Examiner will name the time, signify the speed of the pulse and play the test twice.

Examples: (i)

(ii)

(iv) To recognise modulation from a major key to its dominant or subdominant or from a minor key to its dominant minor or subdominant minor in a short passage played once by the Examiner. The tonic chord will first be sounded.

(v) To name as tonic or dominant and to define as in root position or first inversion a four-part chord in a major key played by the Examiner after he has played the tonic chord in root position.

(vi) To sing or play from memory a melodic phrase of eight or nine notes played twice by the Examiner. The key-chord will first be sounded.

Examples:

Grade VI (Intermediate)

Theory of Music, Grade V (Higher), must have been passed: see pages 12 and 21.

1. Keyboard Tests

(i) To play perfect, plagal, imperfect (I-V) or interrupted cadential progressions either in four-part harmony (three parts in the R.H. and one in the L.H.) or in any free style, at the candidate's choice, in the major keys of C, G, D, F or B♭ and in the minor keys of A, E or D.

(ii) To play *from memory* a piece or section of a piece* not less than 16 bars in length chosen by the candidate from any Grade II album of Pianoforte pieces published by the Board, and then to transpose it from memory into any key chosen by the candidate, at least a whole tone higher or lower than the original.

(iii) To harmonise at sight a simple diatonic melody in the major key of C, G or F. The melody will be in 2/4, 3/4 or 4/4 time and may contain a few passing notes; it can and may be harmonised by chords chosen from the tonic, dominant, subdominant, supertonic and their first inversions, but the candidate need not be limited to using these chords. The candidate may play the melody twice before harmonising it.

Example: 

(iv) To transpose at sight a tone higher or lower:—
either (*a*) a simple diatonic piece of two-part counterpoint written on the treble and bass staves; *or* (*b*) a passage of seven chords (three parts in the R.H. and one in the L.H.) at the candidate's choice.

The candidate may play the test twice in the original key. Major keys only will be used and the original and transposed keys will be limited to 3 sharps or 3 flats (i.e., transposing from key C into key D or B♭; from key D to key C; from key E♭ to F; from key F to E♭ or G; from key G to F or A).

Examples:

Transpose into key D 

Transpose into key F 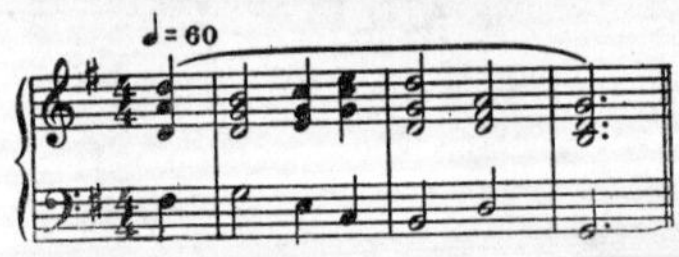

(v) To play from a printed copy a four-bar phrase in simple time written in the major key of C, G or F, and then to continue by adding an answering four-bar phrase, modulating to the dominant.

Example: 

* The candidate must bring a copy of the music for the Examiner's use. The piece may be taken from a book of examination pieces, past or present, or from any of the permanent graded albums.

2. Sight Singing or Sight Playing (at candidate's choice)

Either: To sing at sight a melody which may modulate. The key-chord and first note of the test will be sounded by the Examiner.

Example: 

Or: To play at sight on the pianoforte a test of similar difficulty to the Sight Reading in Pianoforte Grade V.

3. Aural Tests

(i) To recognise perfect, plagal, imperfect (I-V) and interrupted cadential progressions in major and minor keys. The key-chord will be sounded and followed immediately by the two chords forming the progression, played twice by the Examiner.

(ii) To sing or play from memory the lower part of an easy two-part phrase in a major key played twice by the Examiner, the key-chord having been sounded.

Example: 

(iii) (*a*) To clap the rhythm-pattern of a melody played twice by the Examiner; to say whether the time is simple duple, triple or quadruple; and to beat time when the music is repeated by the Examiner.

(*b*) To identify note-values (e.g., as minim, crotchet, quaver, including dotted notes) of a short-time pattern in 2/4, 3/4 or 4/4 played twice by the Examiner who will name the time-signature and signify the speed of the pulse.

(iv) To recognise modulation from a major key to its dominant, sub-dominant, or relative minor or from a minor key to its dominant minor, subdominant minor or relative major in a short passage played once by the Examiner. The tonic chord will first be sounded.

(v) To name as tonic or dominant or subdominant and to define as in root position or first inversion a four-part chord in a major key played by the Examiner after he has played the tonic chord in root position. (N.B.—Second inversions will not be used.)

(vi) To sing or play from memory a melody three or four bars in length played twice by the Examiner. The key-chord and first note of the test will be sounded.

(*a*)  (*b*) 

Grade VII (Advanced)

Theory of Music, Grade V (Higher), must have been passed: see pages 12 and 21.

1. Keyboard Tests

(i) To play perfect, plagal, imperfect (I-V) or interrupted cadential progressions either in four-part harmony (three notes in the R.H. and one in the L.H.) or in any free style, at candidate's choice, in major or minor keys up to four sharps or four flats.

(ii) To harmonise at sight a simple diatonic melody in the major key of C, G, D or F or minor key of A, E, D or C. The melody will be in 2/4, 3/4, 4/4 or 6/8 time and may contain passing notes; it can and may be harmonised by root position and inversions of chords chosen from the tonic, dominant, subdominant, supertonic and submediant and the root position of the dominant seventh, but the candidate need not be limited to using these chords. The candidate may play the melody twice before harmonising it.

Example in major key:

Example in minor key:

(iii) To transpose at sight a simple passage written in four parts (three notes in R.H. and one in L.H.) into the key a tone or semitone higher or lower. The original and transposed keys will not go beyond the keys of four sharps or four flats. The candidate may play the passage once in the original key before transposing it.

Examples:

(*a*) Transpose a semitone lower.

(*b*) Transpose a tone higher.

(iv) To extemporise a short piece from a given opening phrase in the key of C or G major or A minor in dance style (Minuet, Sarabande, Gavotte, etc.). At least one modulation should be introduced. Candidates may, if they wish, extemporise in any other key, in which case they must transpose the given opening phrase into the required key. A printed copy of the opening phrase will be put before the candidate who will be allowed to play it once before attempting the extemporisation.

Examples:

(v) To play at sight a three-part vocal score for Soprano, Alto and Bass, written in two G clefs and one F clef, about eight bars in length.

Example:

2. Sight Singing or Sight Playing (at candidate's choice)

Either: To sing at sight a melody of reasonable difficulty. The key-chord will first be sounded by the Examiner.

Example:

Or: To play at sight on the pianoforte a test of similar difficulty to the Sight Reading in Pianoforte Grade VII.

3. Aural Tests

(i) To recognise cadences in major or minor keys as perfect, plagal, imperfect or interrupted as these occur in a continuous musical sentence, played twice by the Examiner, the key-chord having been sounded.

(ii) To sing or play from memory the lowest part of a short 3-part passage. The compass will not exceed an octave and will be suited to the vocal range of the candidate. The test will begin with the lowest part and will be played three times by the Examiner.

Examples:

(iii) (*a*) To clap the rhythm-pattern of a melody played twice by the Examiner; to say whether the time is simple duple, triple or quadruple; and to beat time when the music is repeated by the Examiner.

(*b*) To identify note-values (e.g., as minim, crotchet, quaver, including dotted notes) of a short time-pattern in 2/4, 3/4, 4/4 or 6/8 played twice by the Examiner, who will name the time-signature and signify the speed of the pulse.

(iv) To name as tonic or dominant or subdominant and to define as in root position or first or second inversion a four-part chord in a major key played by the Examiner after he has played the tonic chord in root position.

(v) To recognise modulation from a major or minor key to any related key in a short passage played once by the Examiner who will name the key and play the tonic chord. The candidate may use one of the technical names listed below or may state the letter-name of the new key. (From a major key to its dominant, subdominant, relative minor, mediant minor or supertonic minor; from a minor key to its dominant minor, subdominant minor, relative major, submediant major or flattened leading-note major.)

(vi) To play from memory four chords in a major key first played by the Examiner. The chords will be limited to those in section (iv) above. The exact position of the first chord, which will be tonic in root position, will be shown to the candidate by the Examiner, who will then play the phrase three times. The candidate will be given credit for reproducing the correct chords even if the *position* of the inner parts is not exact; it is essential for the outside parts to be exact.

Separate syllabuses for each of the following subjects may be obtained from the Board's offices. All applications must state the instrument or subject required.

WIND INSTRUMENTS: Five Grades only, III, IV, V, VI and VIII.

Candidates may offer Flute, Oboe, Clarinet, Bassoon, Horn, Trumpet (or Cornet) or Tenor Trombone.

A new syllabus is issued for 1964.

DOUBLE BASS. In Grades IV to VII only.

HARP. Grades IV to VII only.

CHAMBER MUSIC FOR INSTRUMENTAL ENSEMBLES

In three standards of difficulty, viz:—

Class I—Lower and Higher standard

Class II—Intermediate and Advanced standard

Class III—Final standard

for Piano trios, String trios, quartets, quintets, sextets and octets; and for combinations of Strings and Wind.

CLASS SINGING: Four Grades, numbered I to IV.

GENERAL INSPECTION OF MUSIC

1. Subjects.

(*a*) Instrumental Music, solo or concerted

(*b*) Solo Singing

(*c*) Singing Classes or Choirs

(*d*) Orchestral Classes

(*e*) Classes for Ear Training, Sight Singing, and other studies included in the syllabus for General Musicianship

(*f*) Paper Work. (Written work of the pupils must be available for inspection if required.)

The programme of the inspection will be determined by the school, teacher or choirmaster, who will choose the music and decide which of the above subjects are to be included. A programme should be submitted by the school or teacher at the time of entry, or at latest three weeks before the date fixed for the inspection. The Examiner may ask the pupils questions and test them individually or collectively at his discretion.

2. Place. Inspections will be arranged at Schools, Teachers' Studios or Churches.

3. Entry. Special forms of application must be completed, stating the subjects for inspection and the number of hours required.

4. Fee. One hour (minimum period) £2 2s. 0d.; each succeeding hour or part of hour £1 11s. 6d.

5. Dates of Entry. Application forms with the fees must reach 14 Bedford Square, London, W.C.1, on or before the dates given in Regulation 7 (page 15).

6. Report. No marks or individual results will be issued, but a written Report on the work inspected will be sent to the Principal of the School, to the Teacher, or to the Choirmaster.

GENERAL CERTIFICATE OF EDUCATION EXAMINATION

Music can be taken as a subject for the General Certificate of Education at Ordinary, Advanced or Scholarship level in England and Wales, and for the Scottish Certificate of Education, and for the Northern Ireland Certificates.

The regulations and requirements of the various examining bodies differ in detail; each one issues its own syllabus. Intending candidates should obtain the regulations of the one with which they are concerned, by applying direct to:

***Cambridge Local Examinations Syndicate, Cambridge.**

*Oxford Local Examinations Delegacy, 12 Merton Street, Oxford.

***Oxford and Cambridge Schools Examination Board,**
74 High Street, Oxford,
or 10 Trumpington Street, Cambridge.
Publications from: Cambridge University Press, Bentley House, London, N.W.1.

*London University Entrance and School Examinations Council.
Publications Department, 1 Malet Street (First Floor), London, W.C.1.

***Durham University School Examinations Board,**
8 Sydenham Terrace, Newcastle-upon-Tyne 2.

Associated Examining Board,
29/31 Brechin Place, London, S.W.7.

Joint Matriculation Board
(Universities of Manchester, Liverpool, Leeds, Sheffield and Birmingham),
Publications from: Messrs. John Sherratt & Son, Park Road, Timperley, Altrincham, Cheshire.

Southern Universities' Joint Board for School Examinations
(Bristol, Reading and Southampton),
22 Berkeley Square, Bristol 8.

Welsh Joint Education Committee,
30 Cathedral Road, Cardiff.

Scottish Education Department,
St. Andrew's House, Edinburgh 1.

Ministry of Education of Northern Ireland,
Her Majesty's Stationery Office, 80 Chichester Street, Belfast.

The Associated Board's practical examinations in Grade V or VI are accepted for some purposes by the bodies marked * whose regulations should be consulted.

Theory Grade V Exemptions (*see Regulation 1, page 12*)

Candidates for the Associated Board's Practical Grades VI, VII and VIII may claim exemption from Theory Grade V on producing evidence of having passed in Music at any level in the examination for G.C.E. of one of the above-named bodies, or in the Scottish Certificate of Education Ordinary Grade, or in the Senior Certificate examinations of Northern Ireland (Junior Certificate being accepted only if the candidate has gained 75 per cent. in the written part).

THE ASSOCIATED BOARD SCHOLARSHIPS

The Board offers for competition in April or May 1965

SIX SCHOLARSHIPS

providing free tuition in London at the Royal Academy of Music or the Royal College of Music as the Board may direct, or at the Royal Manchester College of Music or at the Royal Scottish Academy of Music, if the Scholar prefers.

Tenure

Two years from September, 1965, with the possibility of extension at the discretion of the Board.

Qualification for Entry

(*a*) Distinction in a Practical Grade VIII examination (Grade VII in Harp or Double Bass), taken in any School or Centre in Britain and Ireland in 1964, and

(*b*) A Pass in Theory Grade VI, VII, or VIII in 1964 or previously.

Preference will normally be given to candidates whose ages at the time of the competition are as follows:—

Instrumentalists	Between 16 and 20
Singers	Between 18 and 25

The subject of examination for Scholarship can only be that in which the Practical qualifying examination has been passed. Syllabus and entry forms will be sent out automatically in the second half of January, 1965, to those who gained the Practical qualification (see (*a*) above) during 1964.

Full regulations obtainable on application.

Enquiries about admission of students, diploma examinations and applications for diploma syllabuses, prospectuses, etc., should be addressed to the Royal Academy or College concerned:—

The Secretary,
Royal Academy of Music,
Marylebone Road,
London, N.W.1.

The Registrar,
Royal College of Music,
Prince Consort Road,
London, S.W.7.

The Secretary,
Royal Manchester College
of Music,
Devas Street, Oxford Road,
Manchester, 15.

The Secretary,
Royal Scottish Academy
of Music,
St. George's Place,
Glasgow, C.2.

The Board does not supply any music other than its own publications, and cannot guarantee that the set pieces and songs by other publishers will be kept in stock by all local music sellers throughout 1964. In case of difficulty application should be made to the original publishers before it is assumed that any item has run out of print.

Names and addresses of the publishers mentioned in the syllabus are as follows:—

Ascherberg, Hopwood & Crew Ltd., 16 Mortimer Street, London, W.1.
Ashdown, Edwin Ltd., 19 Hanover Square, London, W.1.
Augener Ltd.—*see* Galliard.
Boosey & Hawkes Ltd., 295 Regent Street, London, W.1.
Bosworth & Co. Ltd., 14/18 Heddon Street, London, W.1.
Breitkopf—*see* British & Continental Music Agencies.
British & Continental Music Agencies, 64 Dean Street, London, W.1.
Chappell& Co. Ltd., 50 New Bond Street, London, W.1.
Chester, J. & W. Ltd., 11 Great Marlborough Street, London, W.1.
Cramer, J. B. & Co. Ltd., 139 New Bond Street, London, W.1.
Curwen, J., & Sons Ltd., 29 Maiden Lane, London, W.C.2.
Elkin & Co. Ltd., 160 Wardour Street, London, W.1.
Forsyth Bros. Ltd., 13 Mortimer Street, London, W.1.
Francis, Day & Hunter, 16 Soho Square, London, W.1.
Frederick Harris Music Co. Ltd., 14 Berners Street, London, W.1.
Freeman, H. & C., 95a St. George's Road, Brighton, Sussex.
Galliard Ltd., 148 Charing Cross Road, London, W.C.2.
Hinrichsen Edition Ltd., 10/12 Baches Street, London, N.1.
Leeds Music Ltd., 25 Denmark Street, London, W.C.2.
Lengnick, Alfred, & Co. Ltd., 14 Sheraton Street, Wardour Street, London, W.1.
Mills Music Ltd., Denmark Street, London, W.C.2.
Novello & Co. Ltd., 160 Wardour Street, London, W.1.
Oxford University Press (Music Dept.), 44 Conduit Street, London, W.1.
Paterson's Publications Ltd., 36 Wigmore Street, London, W.1.
Paxton, W., & Co. Ltd., 36 Dean Street, London, W.1.
Peters—*see* Hinrichsen.
Ricordi, G., & Co. Ltd., 271 Regent Street, London, W.1.
Schirmer—*see* Chappell.
Schott & Co. Ltd., 48 Great Marlborough Street, London, W.1.
Stainer & Bell Ltd., 29 Newman Street, London, W.1.
United Music Publishers Ltd., 1 Montague Street, London, W.C.1.
Universal, 2/3 Fareham Street, Dean Street, London, N.1.
Weekes, A. W., & Co. Ltd.—*see* Galliard.
Weinberger, Josef, Ltd., 33 Crawford Street, London, W.1.
Williams, Joseph, Ltd.—*see* Galliard.

GRAMOPHONE RECORDS OF VIOLIN PIECES AND ACCOMPANIMENTS

E.M.I. Records (H.M.V.) have produced two extended-play records of some of the pieces set for Violin Grades III and IV in 1963/4, having on one side a performance by violin and piano and on the other the piano accompaniments alone for practice. The interpretation in these performances is not necessarily the only one acceptable to examiners. Particulars from the Education Dept., E.M.I. Records Ltd., 20 Manchester Square, London, W.1.

PRINTED IN GREAT BRITAIN BY HEADLEY BROTHERS LTD
109 KINGSWAY LONDON WC2 AND ASHFORD KENT